SAINT THOMAS
A Q U I N A S

ST. THOMAS AQUINAS

BEING PAPERS READ AT THE CELEBRATIONS OF THE SIXTH CENTENARY OF THE CANONIZATION OF SAINT THOMAS AQUINAS, HELD AT MANCHESTER, 1924, BY

ÆLRED WHITACRE, O.P.

VINCENT McNABB, O.P.

PROF. A. E. TAYLOR

MONSIGNOR GONNE

PROF. T. F. TOUT

HUGH POPE, O.P.

WIPF & STOCK · Eugene, Oregon

Wipf and Stock Publishers
199 W 8th Ave, Suite 3
Eugene, OR 97401

St. Thomas Aquinas
Being Papers Read at the Celebrations of the Sixth Centenary of the
Canonization of Saint Thomas Aquinas, Held at Manchester, 1924
By Whitacre, Aelred
ISBN 13: 978-1-60608-828-9
Publication date 7/29/2009
Previously published by B. Herder, 1925

CONTENTS

CONTENTS

INTRODUCTORY NOTE

ORDERED by His Holiness, Pope Pius XI,, to hold celebrations in honour of the Sixth Centenary of the Canonisation of St. Thomas Aquinas, the Friars Preachers of the English Province decided that for various reasons they would be better able to hold them fittingly in Manchester than elsewhere.

Accordingly the University authorities were requested to allow us to organise within the University a series of lectures on the main teaching of St. Thomas in philosophy, theology, ethics, mysticism, and biblical interpretation. Through the kindly offices of the Vice-Chancellor, Sir Henry Miers, the Council of the University, on the recommendation of the Faculty of Theology, agreed to our request and lent us the History Theatre.

Further to make the understanding of St. Thomas' teaching more thorough, we asked Professor Tout, the founder of the most important school of historical studies in England, to give an inaugural lecture on the setting of the saint's life. His consent assured us of the success of the whole course. Indeed the crowded audience attending this first lecture forced us to adjourn to the Chemistry Theatre, where the rest of the lectures were given.

It will be seen, therefore, that the thanks of the organisers of the lectures are due to the Vice-Chancellor, to the Council of the University, and to the Faculty of Theology. But they would like also to express their gratitude to Professor Tout, to Professor Taylor whose brilliant lecture

is included in this book, to Mr. H. P. Turner, M.A., L.L.M.,
the Registrar of External Students, and very considerably
to Professor S. Alexander, whose encouragement and
sympathy urged forward the enterprise.

Finally, we desire to leave on record the kindness of
Dr. H. Guppy, Librarian of the Rylands Library, who
exposed in a show case, during the week that the celebrations lasted (May 26–31, 1924), several valuable early
printed editions of St. Thomas' works.

Part of the admirable sermon preached by Rt. Rev.
Monsignor Gonne at the closing of the celebrations in the
Priory Church of St. Sebastian, Pendleton, has been added
to the lectures to form an epilogue.

The Place of St. Thomas Aquinas in History

By T. F. Tout, M.A., F.B.A.,

Professor of History and Director of Advanced Studies in History
in the University of Manchester

WE are met here to celebrate, a year after its time, the sixth hundred anniversary of the canonisation of St. Thomas Aquinas, the supreme glory of the Dominican order, the greatest philosopher and theologian, and the typical intellectualist saint of the whole Middle Ages. Most things that still live among us have their roots in the Middle Ages, and our modern habit of keeping centenaries and jubilees is but, so to say, a laicised offshoot of the ecclesiastical commemorations of that period. Nor is that habit, though capable of excess and abuse, to be lightly condemned. Its value largely depends on the worthiness of the person commemorated, and in the case of St. Thomas there can be no question at all as to his real claim on our regard. It is easy to understand why those to whom St. Thomas is still the great master should wish to do honour to his memory. It is among all things natural that the Order of Preachers, which still upholds the faith and follows the rule of life of its greatest member, should be eager to distinguish such a time by appropriate commemoration. But a great man does not simply appeal to those of his own way of life and thinking. If the scientific study of history is of any value, it should teach all scholars, whatever their views may be, to appreciate the part in history which such a man has played. Accordingly, those who have no claim to direct discipleship should also be glad to take a share in the honouring of one of the foremost names in the history of thought, one of the most characteristic and strongest of the many great men of the

Middle Ages. This university is pledged to an attitude of neutrality in all disputed questions, whether in religion or in politics. Its mission is the diffusion and extension of knowledge, not the cultivation of this or that phase of opinion. It chooses its teachers for their scholarship and power to advance science, regardless of their views on all the fundamental questions which divide the world. It has ever before its eyes the direction of its founder, who, when he claimed that all subjects taught in any university should be included within its sphere, provided that no tests should be imposed and no religious instruction given which was reasonably offensive to the conscience of any student. It is in this spirit that it has cheerfully offered house room to those who have special reason for commemorating the memory of St. Thomas Aquinas, and that some of its teachers, present and past, have gladly joined in the celebration with those who have special insight into his spirit. We do this because Thomas of Aquino was a great man, and we should do the same for any other eminent man who had played a notable part in the thought or action of his time, and had had a mighty influence on posterity.

This is a course of six lectures which treat of various aspects of Thomas' teaching, from an historical and not from a dogmatic point of view. One who has devoted more years than he cares to remember to the history of the Middle Ages may perhaps introduce the series by an endeavour to assess the historical position of the most characteristic and influential of mediaeval teachers. He makes no claim to special knowledge of either philosophy or theology : others better qualified will deal with these subjects in their turn. But an attempt to put the whole man into his historical perspective and bring into a single focus the many aspects of his activity may perhaps be a useful introduction to the more specialised studies of which this is the prelude. We must not lose sight of the oneness of a career which was, at every stage, inspired by a rare unity of purpose.

Wherein lies Thomas' place in history ? We revere him as a man of singular personality, of remarkable holiness, of immense intellect, of vast learning, of enormous output, and of far-reaching influence. He is the saint, the thinker, the scholar, the teacher, one of the greatest minds of all time. It is not enough that Thomas was a man of exalted holiness and elevation of character. There have been such men in all ages, not least in St. Thomas' own time. But Thomas' sanctity is of a special type of its own, a sanctity characteristic of his order and of that of the thirteenth century, which a French scholar has well described as the most 'rationalist' century of the Middle Ages, meaning by that that it made human reason the ultimate criterion of knowledge. Modern men not seldom find a deterrent element in some aspects of mediaeval sanctity, its excessive macerations of the flesh, its over-powering emotionalism, and the atmosphere of miracle and mystery in which it moved. There is little to put such men off in the sanctity of St. Thomas. Though he yields to none in his whole-hearted acceptance of every article of the mediaeval creed, the fervour of his piety, the loftiness of his morality and his ecstatic faith and devotion, he is ever moderate, reasonable and restrained. John XXII. was well advised when he deprecated the necessity of meticulous enquiry into the miracles St. Thomas had wrought. The Pope declared with great truth that the stupendous miracle of St. Thomas was his whole life, and there are few nowadays who will not agree with him. Miracles, indeed, the saint was universally esteemed to have performed. The Middle Ages expected wonders at every hand, and generally found what they were looking for. But we have only to compare the subordination of the miraculous element in the case of St. Thomas with the immense insistence on it in the case of St. Thomas of Canterbury, to see that we have passed from the mystic twelfth century to the rationalistic age of the great scholastics of the thirteenth. It is not only as a saint but as a Dominican saint of the thirteenth century that Thomas

Aquinas must be judged.   Yet of all mediaeval saints he
is one of the most intelligible to moderns.

The thirteenth century was an age of great men and great
movements, the flowering time of mediaeval civilisation
and of the mediaeval Church, whose ideals best express that
civilisation.   Many sided as Thomas was, he well embodies
the leading characteristics of that wonderful period,
and his historical position can only be rightly appraised
by taking these elements into our sympathetic consideration.   He stood in the forefront of the chief movements of
his age.   He was, above all, the good ' religious,' and the
devoted son of his order.   Now the mendicant friars
represent a particularly characteristic thirteenth-century
type of the ' religious ' ideal.   They took the threefold
monastic vow with whole-hearted sincerity, and they
strove to fortify themselves against the special dangers
of the older orders by the rigid extension of the vow of
poverty from renunciation of individual possessions to
the rejection of all corporate wealth.   Yet the Dominican
interpretation of the vow of corporate poverty was very
different from the mystical worship of Lady Poverty by
St. Francis and his stricter disciples.   What to Francis
was the ultimate principle of action was to Dominic and
his following a practical means of realising abstraction
from worldly temptation and the promotion of knowledge
and glory of God and the Church.   Thus even within
the mendicant ranks, there was both a common aim and
a difference of means.   The result was a remarkable di-
versity of character and type, springing naturally enough
from differences of opinion and a consequential element of
antagonism between them.   Yet it is a superficial view
of history that overstresses these divergencies and neglects
the common ground on which the two orders trod.   To
the best men of both societies Thomas Aquinas and Albert
of Cologne were fellow workers in a common cause with
Bonaventura and Peckham.   Just as the occasional fierce
fights and the chronic antagonism of the mediaeval Church
and State leads historians to forget the normal peaceful

co-operation of the ecclesiastical and the civil powers in the daily work of the mediaeval world, so the equally sharp controversies and the normal difference of outlook between the good Franciscan and the good Dominican tend to make us ignore that the two orders habitually worked together in perfect harmony and cordiality.

Aquinas then is a typical saint and a typical ' religious ' saint. But he also represents a type within the type. His ' religion ' is that of the mendicant friars ; not that of the older monastic orders. There is a whole world of difference between his mentality and outlook from that of a St. Anselm or a St. Bernard. But he is almost as different from Francis or Bonaventura as he is from the Benedictine type. His master is St. Dominic, not St. Francis. From this flow the special characteristics of his ideals and work. The Order of Preachers had a different scheme of life from the older monastic orders, and even from the other orders of friars. And it is first of all as an embodiment of the Dominican ideal that St. Thomas would, I feel sure, have wished to be considered. The Dominicans shared with the Franciscans a mission to the world. They were not recluses, abandoning the world for the self-centred solitude of the cloister ; but they were men, living in common with men like-minded with themselves, so as to gain further strength for co-operation in work to make the world better. The special mission of the Dominicans was an intellectual one. Called into existence to win back southern France from the Albigensian heresy, the functions of the order were to preach, to teach and to study. That its teaching might be based upon sound foundations, its special business was to promote theological and philosophical study. This brought it into the closest contact with the intellectual movements of the time.

In the early thirteenth century all Europe was astir with restless activity. It was a time of great men and movements, new and old. On the strictly religious side the most important thing was the rise of the mendicant orders. On the intellectual side the leading feature of the age was the growth of those societies of teachers and students which were now beginning to be called universities. The establishment of some sort of order had made the life of study once more possible in western Europe. The earliest schools had been occasionally in the palaces of kings, but more normally in the cloisters of certain monasteries. In the second half of the twelfth century it was possible for learning to desert the cloister for the world. Hence great ' secular ' schools grew up at Paris, at Bologna, at Oxford which made the life of study attractive to wider circles. In calling these schools ' secular ' I use the word in its mediaeval sense of ' non-monastic.' All learning was still in clerical hands and, outside Italy, all students and teachers were tonsured clerks, enjoying all the privileges of the clergy, whether they were ordained or not. As these schools increased in numbers, the teachers— called indifferently doctors, masters or professors—formed clubs, or trades unions, according to the different faculties, or groups of subjects, which they studied. These organisations, spontaneous at first, acquired recognition from Church and State, and privileges which made them largely self-governing and self-sufficing. The earliest universities grew, but by the early thirteenth century they were beginning to be created. A pope set up a university at Toulouse; an emperor at Naples. Kings and princes soon began to follow their example.

All Europe was still a single community, closely bound together by the authority of the Church, whose unity was symbolised in the papacy, the ultimate source of all ecclesiastical authority on earth. But the modern nations were not yet in being, and the Church and the university were the last institutions to respond to the national stimulus ; all learning was still international ; all universities had the same language, Latin, and all nations had the same ideals, studies and methods. A scholar could wander freely from one country to another and seek the instruction he desired from the best masters of his subject. The State was, like the Church, theoretically one, but the

Roman Emperor was still supposed to wield the sword temporal, just as the Roman Pope really wielded the sword spiritual. In practice political power had been split up among a crowd of petty feudal princes, who were now being brought together under great monarchs who were gradually building up national states on the ruins of feudalism.

With all his idealism, mediaeval man was a very practical person, and had a keen eye to what would pay. In the realm of learning there consequently arose a danger lest the study of law should absorb too large a share of attention, because law opened up the most attractive worldly career, even to ecclesiastics. The great Italian university of Bologna became primarily a school of law. Philosophy and theology had its chief centre in Paris, and there a different danger arose. The growing curiosity of western scholars was being fed by the study of Latin literature and Greek philosophy, pagan in origin and temper. The popular heresy of the Albigenses, against which St. Dominic founded the order of preachers, might well have its counterpart in every university centre. The study of Aristotle, at first known only by Latin translations derived from Mohammedan sources, was eagerly pursured : but excited general alarm lest it should prove antagonistic to Christian philosophy. It was the mission of the Dominicans to reconcile Greek thought with Christian theology. To effect this purpose they had to take up their quarters in university towns, and where universities were lacking, set up universities, *studia generalia*, of their own. In all these Dominican schools they expounded to swarms of scholars their doctrine that the thought of the ancient world was the best schoolmaster to bring men to Christ and His Church. The greatest, though not the first, of the brethren who carried through this task was St. Thomas Aquinas. He is academic as much as he is monastic. He is the teacher, thinker and writer above all things.

Such was the religious, political and intellectual environment of the great Dominican saint. Let us next glance at his personal surroundings, including some brief sketches of the turning points of his singularly serene and well-ordered life.

It is a cherished illusion that the mediaeval scholar was a humble person, of little social estimation, who supported himself in his youth by begging and later on by the favours of the great. That a poor man could become a scholar is eminently to the credit of the time, but it is still more creditable that the career of learning was attractive to all classes of the community, and that men were found from the highest to the lowest willing to dedicate themselves to so unremunerative and laborious a career. St. Thomas was himself a man of the highest birth, a scion of a great feudal family in the northern part of the kingdom of Naples. The traveller by train from Rome to Naples will, when nearly half way on his journey, pass down the rich valley of the Liri where the house of Aquino's chief estates lay. He will see from the window castles crowning the craggy hills encompassing the vale. It was in such castles that the saint was born and passed his early years. One station is Roccasecca, dominated by the stronghold in which Thomas first saw the light. The next is Aquino, from which his family derived their name and title. The next is Casino, towering over which is the lofty hill on the top of which is perched the famous monastery of Monte Casino, where he received his early schooling. All these places are within a few miles of each other : the traveller must now go some 70 miles farther before he reaches the great city of Naples, where Thomas' early adolescence was spent, where he studied arts at the infant university recently established by Frederick II., which only a few weeks ago celebrated the seventh centenary of its foundation. It was at Naples, too, that Thomas, to the disgust of his kinsfolk, renounced a worldly career to enter the order of St. Dominic. Before long, however, personal and political troubles made the Dominican convent at Naples a difficult place for him. His promise made him widely known at an incredibly early age, so that the head of the order, John the Teutonic, thought it prudent to take him away with him from his native land, and to escort him over the Alps to Paris and thence to Cologne, where the most eminent of the first generation of Dominican philosophers, Albert, called the Great, a German of birth equal to that of Thomas, was now directing a famous Dominican school. Of this teacher and school Thomas became the most distinguished disciple, and was destined to carry out more completely and effectively that system of philosophical theology which Albert had begun.

We have seen that from the beginning the Dominicans sought out the university centres. Dominic himself ended his days at Bologna, and in that city the shrine of the sainted founder still remains. In northern France and in England the first Dominican houses were at Paris and Oxford. But there was no university, either then or for the rest of St. Thomas' life, in Germany. Accordingly Cologne, though a Dominican *studium generale*, was not a university school. However, the teaching of Albert the Great made it an adequate place of education for the greatest of the Dominican scholastics. While Thomas was engaged upon his studies at Cologne, difficulties arose between his order and the established universities. The troubles were natural enough and neither the universities nor the Dominicans can wholly bear the blame for them. The 'secular' doctors, who controlled the Paris schools, looked askance on the friars because they neither conformed to university traditions nor accepted current university teaching. A Dominican *studium generale* in a university town tended to become a rival university to the established academic centre. The Dominican masters in such schools claimed an independence for themselves that ran athwart all the trade union rules; they were 'blacklegs' who wanted free trade in teaching for men who had not gone through the recognised academic courses, but had received their training in the schools attached to Dominican or Franciscan convents. For from the beginning the mendicants did not think the university courses were sufficient for their needs. They set up elaborate schools in their own convents in the university towns, and sometimes in other places, as for example at Cologne. They could educate their pupils so well that it was clearly a waste of time for them to go through their preliminary arts course again at the university. They demanded to study theology from the beginning of their entrance, and were not even careful that their theological teachers were divinity graduates of the university. Up to this point the universities had been non-monastic, that is to say ' secular ' societies. They were now threatened with an invasion of the new type of ' religious,' whose ideal was not cloistered seclusion but study and learning. In answer to this, the ' secular ' doctors retaliated by refusing the licence to teach to all who had not followed the normal university curriculum. When, on one occasion, the University of Paris was in such fierce conflict with other enemies that it had recourse to the true trades' union remedy of a strike, it had a new grievance against the friars that they went on with their teaching, despite the solemnly proclaimed ' cessation ' of all lectures. There was some reason for complaint against teachers who accepted the privileges of the university without submitting to its authority. To remedy it the university required an oath of obedience to its decrees from all who practised in its schools, and expelled the friars for disobeying the new statutes. Luckily for the friars, the Pope was then Alexander IV., a great patron of their orders. In 1255 he decided most of the disputed points in favour of the mendicants, and ordered the university to admit to the mastership as many duly qualified candidates as he thought fit. The university did its best to resist, but was in the long run compelled to accept the position. Finally, a sort of compromise was established by which the friars' convents in the university towns became, so to say, universities within the university. It was the beginning of the ' collegiate ' system which has still strangely survived in the two old universities of England, though it has long ago died a natural death upon the Continent. Though open to the fundamental objection of splitting up the teaching resources of the university into various small exclusive societies, not always strong enough to give its pupils the best instruction that might be had, it had some real advantages, notably in the way of discipline, organisation and social amenities. For the Dominicans, it saved them from the danger of their schools becoming rivals to the university. It secured them a firm foothold within the university, while allowing them still to live their own life in their own convents, and order things there as they would.

During this struggle between seculars and mendicants Thomas and his master Albert were transferred from Cologne to Paris. Paris was the one great centre of theological learning for all Europe. It was only at Paris, therefore, such stars could shine with all their natural splendour, that the fullest career could accrue to the most gifted of mendicant philosophers. It was during the very thick of the fight that Thomas went through his theological course at Paris, and it was immediately at the end of it that in 1256 he became a doctor of divinity with the right and obligation to teach his science to others. Some trouble was clearly anticipated from the secular doctors, for the Pope thought it worth while to send an express mandate to the Chancellor to admit him to his degree. Before the order arrived, the university had done this on its own account. Thomas' troubles were now over, and from 1256 to 1261 he remained at Paris as a regent master, what we should call a professor, of theology. He was one of the leaders at the general chapter of the order in 1259, which ordained that readers, that is Dominican professors of theology, should not be troubled by offices or business which involved their withdrawal from lecturing and study. He himself fully profited by this freedom. It was in those years began his great reputation as a teacher and writer, so that very soon the university, which had nearly spurned him, owed an increase in its fame to the possession of a professor of world-wide reputation. We owe it to Alexander IV. that the saint so easily obtained this establishment.

Only eighteen years of life were still before the young professor, but those years were comparatively smooth. He was still bound by his double allegiance to the university and to his order, and in the case of a conflict of authority, it was the order not the university that gained the day. The result was that in 1261 Thomas was recalled to Italy : though this change in no wise interrupted his course of life but rather gave him more leisure for his own personal work. He still taught, sometimes possibly at Bologna, more notably in the 'University of the Papal Court,' an anomalous and peripatetic university which followed the Pope in his constant wanderings, and was then more often in some upland town in central Italy, at Viterbo, at Orvieto, at Perugia than at Rome itself. The inconvenience of migration was compensated for by the advantage of teaching and preaching to the constant crowd from all parts of Christendom that had occasion to visit the head-quarters of the Church Universal. At last a chapter of the province in 1265 ordered Thomas to 'keep school' at Rome with power to send back to their convents idle or negligent brethren.

Those years were for Thomas a time of ever increasing activity. He now wrote his *Summa contra Gentiles*, a comparatively short and non-technical epitome of his theological and philosophical doctrine. But Paris was after all the intellectual centre of the Church, though the Papal Court was its administrative and legal centre. There was loss as well as gain in Thomas' removal from the greatest of the mediaeval universities.

In 1269 Thomas was again transferred to the Paris schools, and taught there for a second period of nearly three years. Recalled to Italy in 1272, despite the protests and entreaties of the Parisian masters, the provincial chapter allowed him to hold a 'general school of theology' at such place with such fellow workers and such a number of students as

he thought fit. It is significant that he at once went back
to his old home in the Dominican convent at Naples.
His teaching remained primarily addressed to Dominicans,
but it is probable that he also taught at the university
there which Charles of Anjou, King of Naples and Sicily
since 1265, had galvanised into some sort of life. However,
Thomas' great preoccupation now was not teaching, but
the composition of his great *Summa Theologica* by which
he will always be remembered. His absorption in this
was diminished by indifferent health, but he had made
immense progress when the call of duty once more sum-
moned him over the Alps. Pope Gregory X. had con-
voked a General Council to meet at Lyons in 1274 in order
to settle the troubles of Christendom and in particular
to devise terms for the reconciliation of the Orthodox
Church of the East with the Catholicism of the West.
The Pope wished to be supported by the best theological
opinion, and called to his help not only St. Thomas, but
Bonaventura, general of the Franciscans and cardinal.
With a heavy heart Thomas made his way northwards,
filled with forebodings as to the future and grieved beyond
measure that he had already found some diminution in his
power of work and in his failure to bring to a completion
his great *Summa*. His faithful *socius*, a simple unlearned
soul, sought to cheer him by expatiating on the great
position that he would have in the Council, that he would
be like Bonaventura, a cardinal, the arbiter of Christendom.
But worldly advancement had never any charm for the
great scholastic, who only desired leisure and health to
finish the book on which his whole mind was set. However,
he made his way northwards through the scenes familiar
in his childhood, and tarried for a time in a castle, owned
by the husband of his sister. There he was smitten by a
grievous sickness, and brought near to death. He now
wished to end his days not among soldiers and nobles,
but among men of religion, and at his earnest request was
moved with difficulty to the neighbouring Cistercian
abbey of Fossa Nova, a beautiful early Gothic building,

planted in the wilderness amidst the desolate and malarious Pontine marshes. Here he took to his bed and died, when not more than 48 years of age. The visitor of Fossa Nova can still see the ancient buildings of the monastery, the very room in which the saint expired, and the beautiful church in which his remains were first laid. But it was not thought right that the body of so great a luminary of the Friars Preachers should remain permanently in the house of another religious order, and ultimately it found an appropriate translation to the great church of Toulouse, the city where Dominic had begun the work which Thomas had brought to complete fruition.

We are fortunate in possessing enough material to enable us to know what manner of man St. Thomas really was. He is described as a tall man, with a big head, inclined to baldness, and brown in complexion. His physical strength must have been as great as his intellectual capacity. His life was of the utmost simplicity and ordered as that of a good religious should be. He began the day by saying mass and by attending subsequently another mass celebrated by another priest. He spent the greater part of his morning in lecturing, and when not teaching, in study and writing in his cell. He wrote, as he celebrated, with tears of ecstatic devotion, and with a constant sense of his unworthiness. 'What I have written,' he said, 'are but trifles, straws, vanities.' At Naples he was rarely seen outside the cloister of his convent. He was content with one or two simple meals a day, taking no thought as to what he ate or drank, or wore. The only record of any personal preference in matters of food is the story that on his death bed he expressed a wish to eat a fresh herring, a delicacy not obtainable by natural means on the coasts of the Mediterranean. He was solitary in temper, absent-minded and abstracted in society. Though a great preacher and lecturer, he never spoke an unnecessary word. But his personal magnetism inspired in his pupils and brethren an absolutely unlimited devotion. A man of the highest social rank, he associated as an equal with kings and princes ; and he was as simple and natural when the guest of St. Louis as when he was in his daily life in the convents of his own order.

Thomas was a prodigious worker ; he had read and absorbed all the science and learning of his age, and had classified it all with the rigorous method which he applied to his own works. His output was enormous. The best known editions of his collected works take up seventeen and nineteen large folio volumes, and of the twelve folios of the unfinished edition, projected by Leo XIII., no less than nine are required to contain the *Summa Theologica*. This mass of work is partly to be accounted for by his extraordinary assiduity, and partly by his wonderful power of absorption and concentration. And what he said was closely reasoned, worked out logically and methodically on a prearranged plan and qualified by references and quotations which shewed that he had made his own the whole of the literature, sacred and profane, accessible to his age. It is said that he could keep three or even four amanuenses busily employed in taking down in writing the stream of words that flowed from his lips. The forebodings that preceded his death were based on the feeling that he would have to leave the world before he had accomplished all that he had in his mind to do. For with all his productiveness he left unfinished a good deal of his work. But ardent disciples were always at hand who eagerly strove to complete what the master had been unable to accomplish. This was the easier since he had worked out most of his schemes in the form of academic lectures, which his pupils had taken down as they heard them delivered. We may perhaps discount the amount of his work, and largely account for its bulk by the cir-cumstance that so much of it is the result of oral exposition in the class room. How many folios could not most academic teachers perpetrate if they had at their feet a swarm of devoted pupils who elaborated and published the notes of all the lectures they had attended ! And modern impatience has reduced the normal lecture to the span of a brief hour or fifty minutes, which the lecturer exceeds at his peril. The mediaeval mind had a less meticulous regard for time. Lecture hours were fixed not by the clock, but by the intervals between one canonical hour and another, which varied with the season of the year. It is clear that three hours was not an impossible time for a lecture to last, and that they were normally nearer two hours than one. A reported lecture of such prodigious length would be almost the equivalent of a modern volume. But the main difference would still remain that few of the best impromptus of the class room could have stood the test of time like the prelections of the angelic doctor. And there still remains the prodigious fact that this great productiveness represents an academic career of less than twenty years. Herein lies, as the Pope so truly said, the greatest miracle worked by the saint.

The range of Thomas' work was as surprising as its mass. It was still an age when modern specialisation was unthought of, when a scholar might without presumption take all knowledge for his province; but it may be doubted whether any man, save his master, Aristotle, ever mastered and digested all the encyclopaedia of the sciences better than did the Dominican scholastic. Some aspects of his varied activities will be revealed to you by experts in the course of lectures of which this makes the beginning. You will be told of the teaching of St. Thomas as a philosopher, as a theologian, as a moralist, as a mystic and as an expositor of Holy Scripture; and you will doubtless be informed of the great value of his contributions to all these subjects. Yet they are only selected specimens, so to say, of his point of view. Thomas' particular contribution to the building up of the mediaeval university ideal, Thomas as university teacher and as a preacher, Thomas as a poet and a hymn writer, Thomas as a political philosopher and as an economist, Thomas as a personal influence, Thomas' place in the history of the friars and in the history of his own order, Thomas as a saint, Thomas' attitude to the world in which he

lived and his influence in action : all these would have
been excellent subjects for further illustration and exposition. Yet the more we split up our study of Thomas
into sections, the more we are in danger of losing sight of
the coherent harmony of the Thomist philosophy as a
whole, and of its correspondence with the character of
the author. We cannot draw deep lines separating the
various elements of Thomas' doctrine. It was all inspired by a common purpose. This purpose was in a word
the reconciliation of reason and revelation, the proof that
the wisdom of the Greeks was the training for the teaching
of the Church, the preparation for the Gospel. His method
is as rationalistic as that of Abelard and would, I imagine,
have provoked the indignation of St. Bernard almost as
much as did the methods of Abelard. He is ever ready to
recognise that reason is the dominating factor in all human
activity, ' ratio autem in homine habet locum dominantis.'
His ideal is to prove everything, to take nothing on trust.
He states every objection fairly and clearly ; he always
argues and never denounces ; he has a curious tolerance
and mildness in dealing with those from whom he differs.
When he composes his *Summa contra Gentiles*, a comparatively short compendium of his doctrine, his attitude to
the ' heathen ' with whom he is pleading is that of
persuasion not that of denunciation. He is out to convince, and he considers the right method of conviction is
the recognition of what is essentially sound in his opponents' point of view. For Thomas, even the Jew has his
place in the economy of the Universe. The Jews may
follow their rites, for these rites foreshadow Christian
truth. Their children must not be baptized against their
parents' wishes, for an unwilling convert is a danger to
the faith, and it is wrong to undermine the rights of a father
to control his own children. Other unbelievers may be
tolerated when toleration is the best way of avoiding evil.
Heretics deserve death, but the Church looks to the con-
version of the wanderers, and must aim at convincing them
of error rather than at proceeding hot-headedly to the

punishment of their crime. Unbelief is not inconsistent
with dominion, for heathen rulers have dominion according
both to human law and the law of nations. The Middle
Ages were not tolerant, and no one would claim that
toleration was an invariable quality of the order which
organised and controlled the Inquisition. But the intellectual tolerance running through the chief works of
Thomas, puts him at opposite poles to the fanatical zealot,
who sweeps away all opposition by violence of denunciation
and action.

St. Thomas' receptivity to non-Christian teaching is
best shewn by his whole-hearted devotion to the doctrine
of Aristotle. To him, as to his intellectual disciple Dante,
Aristotle is ' the Philosopher,' the great authority on all
subjects which have to be settled by human intelligence.
Just as Virgil, another heathen teacher, is Dante's guide
to the nether world, so is the heathen philosopher, Aristotle,
Thomas' guide to the solution of all the problems of the
world of thought and reason in which we live. On physics
and on metaphysics, on logic and on morals, on politics
and on economics, Aristotle has always the last word.
In Thomas' youth the schools were still in doubt whether
Aristotle, and his Arab and Jewish interpreters, were not
a wholly reprehensible influence, whose writings were to
be condemned, and whose expositors were to be driven
from the schools. The battle for Aristotle had already
been fought and won before Thomas had become a doctor,
and no one had done more for the Greek sage than Thomas'
famous master Albert. But the Aristotle that Thomas
knew was at least the real Aristotle, as real an Aristotle
as could be found by a generation that only knew Greek
as a commercial language, useful for trading in the Near
East. Another guide was Plato, as worthy of respect to
Thomas as to Aristotle, but there was suspected to be
lurking in Plato an element of unbalanced mysticism
which had upon occasion wrecked his followers on the
rocks and shoals of error and excess. However, neither
Aristotle nor Plato nor even Augustine were enough ;

they had to be supplemented by the teaching of the Gospel and by the authority of the Church. But there was no incompatibility between the teaching of the Philosopher, properly interpreted, and the doctrine of Christ. Philosophy was the school master which brought men to the Church, and in the combination of Greek reason and Christian faith lay the highest wisdom. It is in this spirit that Thomas surveys the whole field of knowledge. Coming towards the creative and living period of mediaeval speculation, he stands to his world as Aristotle stood to the Greek world. In this spirit he strove to interpret and explain nature, society and divinity as a whole.

It was a colossal undertaking and its completion was beyond the power even of St. Thomas. But his wonderful power of concentration on the work which he regarded as specially his own, enabled him to make a real attempt to cover this enormous field. Those who know that without whole-hearted dedication to the great task no real progress in knowledge is possible, will best be able to admire the single-minded devotion with which Thomas refused to turn either to the right or to the left in any direction that led him from his main purpose. A Dominican scholar had the initial advantage over both his monastic and secular colleagues that he belonged to a society that recognised study and learning as having a primary call on the devotion of its members. It is true that he had above all things the duty of preaching, and Thomas preached not only because preaching was incumbent on all members of the order of preachers. He was among the great preachers of the day when the pulpit was the more influential because in an age of few books and no widespread literary knowledge sermons were the most potent way of influencing men's minds. They were the more potent because they were comparatively rare, because preaching was not a duty incumbent on every priest, whether he could preach or not, but was reserved for trained experts and specialists, such as was every member of the order of preachers. The Dominican was

not, like the Benedictine, forced to a rule of life that
employed his time and strength in the routine of devotion.
He was not, like the good secular clerk, absorbed in the
cure of souls, or in the government of the Church. He had
the leisure for literary pursuits and the solitude and the
material and personal help necessary for their application.
He had not, like the modern professor or clergyman, to
respond to the enormous demands on his time and energy
which administration, committee work, the serving of
tables throw upon them.[1]   Indeed it was the absence of
modern fussiness and business distractions that account
for the wonderful way in which the mediaeval scholar
was able to live the scholar's life of producing a worthy
contribution towards the advancement of knowledge,
despite his lack of all the mechanical aids to learning that
modern conditions now allow.   He had never to face the
distractions involved in the call of a career, in the pursuit
of professional advancement.   But the demands of the world
on the Church were in some ways as subtle and insistent
as they are nowadays.   The Church was the greatest of
institutions, the most complicated of administrative
machines.   The cares of the government of the Church
combined with the large share they took in the government
of the state to divert churchmen from spiritual to administrative functions.

Even the Dominican order was not exempt from these
temptations, and Thomas had, if he would, plenty of
legitimate opportunities of deserting his real work.   The
service of the order was an obvious claim ; but though
Thomas did his duty in attending chapters, general and
provincial, he never so much as became prior of the house
to which he was attached, still less a provincial prior or
the general of his order.   But friars were now being raised
to the highest posts in the Church.   In Thomas' youth his

---

[1] I cannot resist quoting a statute of the general chapter of 1259 at Valen-
ciennes, inspired by Thomas and Albert.   It ordered ' quod lectores non
occupentur in officiis vel negotiis per que a lectionibus vel disputationibus
retrahantur.'—Douais, *Acta Capitulorum Provincialium Ordinis Predica-
torum, 1239-1302*, p. 88.   Compare *Cart. Univ. Paris.* I. 385.

master Albert had been persuaded to become Bishop
of Ratisbon, and before he died, his opponent, Robert
Kilwardby, became Archbishop of Canterbury. It is true
that after a brief period Albert withdrew from his see to his
convent and took up with fresh zest his life as a teacher,
and that the great primate ceased to contribute to the
extension or spread of knowledge. Thomas might have
been Archbishop of Naples, but he refused all such pre-
ferment, and died a simple friar. He had no objection
on principle to friars holding high offices in the Church,
and drew up wise rules for their guidance in such cases.
But he recognized that acceptance of such posts would
mean that he could not carry out the task that he was best
qualified to perform. Thus he escaped the lot of a Bonaventura, a Peckham or a Kilwardby, diverted from study
by the duties of high church office, the generalship of his
order, the college of Cardinals, or a great see like that of
Canterbury. In the same spirit Thomas kept aloof from
politics. He was no Bernard, making popes and directing
kings from his convent ; but he kept a shrewd eye on the
political outlook. Had he been a mere unworldly recluse,
he could not have made his important contribution to
the theory of the mediaeval state.

We must not, however, imagine that Thomas was
without honour and influence in his own days. But his
authority was based upon conditions hardly possible
before the thirteenth century. He represents the new type
made possible by the rise of the universities and by the
close intellectual co-operation between them and the
mendicant orders. He is perhaps the first university
professor—to translate his position into modern language—
who exercised a world-wide influence on thought and even
on affairs. The type is not even now particularly common,
and is still almost unthinkable in this country of ours.
It was, however, significant of the most intellectualist
century of the Middle Ages that Thomas should so early
have won his great position. It is not less significant
that the most intellectualist of the religious orders should

have developed the sublimation of this particular type.
A real advance in civilisation is involved when a leader
of thought could thus become a leader of men. Even
now, how far are we from Plato's vision of a state when
kings are philosophers and philosophers kings ? It is
for that reason particularly appropriate that we of the
universities should do such as in us lies to cherish the
memory of the first great saint of Christendom whose
whole life was that of a university teacher and whose
greatest work was a profound system of philosophy.

A leader of thought in an age of restless intellectual
ferment must excite opposition. Accordingly Thomas
was engaged in controversy for almost the whole of his
working career. There were the struggles against the
external enemies of the faith, the Mohammedans, the
Jews and the outspoken heretics. There was the controversy between the secular and the mendicant doctors
within the University to which I have already referred.
There was the incompatibility of spirit between Dominican
intellectualism and Franciscan mysticism, between the
philosophy and the poetry of the faith. Besides taking
his share in all these Thomas had to maintain the position
of the orthodox and Catholic Aristotelian against those
unbalanced Aristotelians of the following of the Arab,
Averroes, who emphasized the incompatibilities between
the peripatetic doctrine and orthodoxy and invited the
condemnation of the Church by a scarcely veiled pan-
theism or agnosticism. He had a more subtle contention
with the school which long held the first place in reputation,
which had resisted Aristotelian influence under the inspiration of a Platonic or rather pseudo-platonic idealism,
such as had of old been a main source of the teaching of
St. Augustine. This trouble was the more difficult since in
Thomas' lifetime Thomism could not even command
universal acceptance within the Dominican order, and
the Augustinian point of view was upheld not only by
Franciscans, such as Bonaventura and Peckham, but by
so prominent a Dominican as Robert Kilwardby, Peckham's

predecessor in the see of Canterbury and afterwards cardinal bishop of Porto. It is a proof of the intellectual independence of the age of St. Thomas that orders, each with a distinct atmosphere of its own, were divided into opposite camps on these fundamental problems of speculation. If the Dominican Kilwardby joined hands with the Franciscans in regarding with suspicion the philosophy of Albert and Thomas, the pioneer of Catholic Aristotelianism was Alexander of Hales, the English doctor of the Paris schools, who a generation earlier had entered the Franciscan order in the very height of his reputation, and devoted his later teaching to the making smooth the way which Albert and Thomas were later to traverse.

It was a noteworthy feature of St. Thomas that in a life of controversy he always shewed the utmost consideration and courtesy to his opponents. The public disputations, which were the stimulus and the glory of the mediaeval academic mind, involved conditions eminently unfavourable to a calm and unbiassed consideration of the questions under dispute. It was the glory of St. Thomas that he never lost his temper or his suavity in the heat of the most strenuous of debates. One of his admirers tells us how ' in public disputations, in which men are sometimes wont to go beyond the bounds of discretion, Thomas was always moderate, meek, humble and considerate, indulging in no glorious or swelling phrase and behaving with extreme politeness to his adversaries.' On one occasion a disputation was held in the Paris schools between Thomas and John Peckham, the protagonists of the new and the old philosophies. Peckham was a pompous, ' donnish,' self-important personage, who wrote and spoke in a very inflated and grandiloquent style, and must have been a most irritating individual with whom to carry on a controversy. Peckham on this occasion assailed Thomas ' with swelling and sounding words ' and ' exasperated the said Thomas.' ' Yet never did Thomas lose his temper, but always answered the said

John with kindness and suavity. And the same thing the said Thomas did in all disputations, however acute and heated they became.'[1] In the fifty years between Thomas' death and canonisation, it was still a disputed question how far certain aspects of his teaching were sound, though there was no disagreement as to his learning, his commanding intelligence and his singleness of purpose. The questions which a few years before had been in debate between Thomas and Peckham still remained undecided. We have the testimony of Peckham himself, who, despite his faults of manner, was a high-minded and conscientious man, as to what was the result of the debate.[2] In written, though not in spoken controversy, he could maintain his courtesy, though he could never drop into a simple method of expressing himself. 'Friar Thomas of Aquino of holy memory,' wrote Peckham, ' in my presence humbly submitted his opinions to the balance and file of the Parisian masters of theology; these opinions still remain before the Roman court undecided.' When within four years of Thomas' death his chief opponent within his own order, Archbishop Kilwardby, was raised from the see of Canterbury to the cardinal bishopric of Porto, there was a strong influence in the Roman curia adverse to a decision in his favour. When Peckham was, by papal provision, made Kilwardby's successor at Canterbury, another opponent of Thomism was established in a great position in the Church. A third antagonist was found in Stephen Tempier, Bishop of Paris, who drew up a series of articles, sometimes looked upon as condemnatory of the teaching of St. Thomas, and strove to impose them upon the great university of which he was diocesan. Peckham laboured, with zeal only equalled by his tactlessness, to follow up the similar policy to that which Kilwardby had adopted as regards Oxford. Yet within a few years the Dominican order was, to Peckham's

---

[1] *Acta Sanctorum* (Bollandist) March, I., 712.

[2] *Reg. Ep. J. Peckham*, III., 866, 871. This **was** written ten years after Thomas' death, and probably fifteen years after the disputation.

indignation, proclaiming that the opinions of Thomas were
the official opinions of the whole order. Even Peckham,
however, had to distinguish between the general teaching
of Thomas and the more uncompromising doctrines of the
Averroistic school against which the blasts of Tempier
and Kilwardby were primarily directed.

  Gradually the debate shifted to broader issues, and
within a generation or so the opinions of Thomas were
accepted as the opinions of the whole Church. This was
particularly the case with the real issue underlying the
disputes of the schools. This was whether reason was the
ally of religion or its natural enemy. The question involved the whole problem of the relations of Christian
to non-Christian philosophy. Since the days of the early
fathers there had been a continual succession of Christian
advocates who declared, in the seventh century with St.
Gregory the Great, and in the twelfth century with St.
Bernard of Clairvaux, that heathen literature and heathen
philosophy were dangerous snares to the faithful. There
was an opposite school who maintained that Christianity
was but the fulfilment of the philosophies, just as the
Gospel was the fulfilment of the Jewish law. St. Augustine
made a powerful contribution in this direction, and
Augustine's influence on early scholasticism, notably on
St. Anselm, had remained a dominant one in the schools
until the days of Bonaventura, and ever remained a far
from negligible element in Thomas' own teaching. But
it was in the long run no longer the decisive influence.
When Thomas had embodied in his *Summa* the leading
metaphysical, logical and even the ethical conceptions of
Aristotle, and had woven them into his great system of
Catholic philosophy, he had set the tone to the main
current of religious thought for many centuries. Philosophy was no longer the avowed foe of theology. Reason
was no longer the enemy of religion. Reason was divine
and religion was rational. All knowledge must be
examined by the intelligence and brought into a harmo-
nious and coherent system. Christian belief must be

c

rationalized, if it is to be communicable or intelligible. To ask questions on high matters is not a temptation of the devil, but the natural right of every thinking man. All ' rationalism ' does not necessarily lead to negative results. So long as religion remains a power, the Thomist approach to it may well still hold the field. Even if, as some say, religion ceases to have its hold upon the thinking mind, the rationalism of St. Thomas will still be among the great heritages of the intellectual world. Apart from the Christian field the Thomist approach to philosophy will still need consideration, just as much as is the case with the doctrine of Aristotle or Kant. Not only Thomists or Catholics or Christians, but all thinking men must recognize Thomas' permanent place in history.

This predominance of Thomist opinion was much strengthened by the movement which resulted in Thomas' canonisation within less than fifty years of his death. We may pause for a moment to consider this movement, since it brings us across a remarkable aspect, only too seldom considered, of the activity of the much decried popes who ruled the Church from Avignon. The fourteenth century, which was covered by their activity, was throughout Europe a great period of administrative reconstruction. The princes of Europe were ordering their states after a more elaborate fashion, and from their efforts rose the beginnings of the modern national state. The same process of administrative definition, which was giving increased efficiency and better order to every political organisation in the West, was also being applied to the government of the Church. Here the world ideal was still a reality. It was the special work of the Avignon popes to bring about the completion of this process. We are here only concerned with one small aspect of it, namely the perfection of the method of the canonisation of saints into an orderly judicial system, conducted under the direct guidance of the papacy. From a very early age of the Church the Christian reverence for martyrs and confessors had led to the paying of special honour to their memory. The method by which such special sanctity and cultus were recognized was called canonisation. Canonisation at first was a very informal and local affair, and there was no universal standard or tribunal. The result was great varieties of local observance and great uncertainty as to which saints were to be honoured. Evils arose from this indefiniteness, and the remedy for them was found in a centralising movement which made the papacy the ultimate tribunal in questions of canonisation. Evidence is lacking to determine all the stages of this process, but we can with certainty trace it back to the tenth century. It was immensely strengthened when Urban II., the preacher of the First Crusade, laid down the general principle that no one should be admitted to the canon of saints, save on sure ocular testimony as to his life and miracles and with the assent of a full council. The last stage of the process was when Alexander III. pronounced that no one, however holy, should be canonised without direct papal authority.

The results of this establishment of the papacy as the sole tribunal in cases of canonisation is well illustrated by the history of the British saints. There is only evidence that two pre-Conquest saints of the British Islands, whether Celtic or English, received formal canonisation from the Pope. Among those not so recognised were names, both Celtic and English, so universally honoured as Patrick of Ireland, David of Wales and Dunstan of Canterbury, and our northern saints, Chad and Bede. The only exceptions were Edward the Confessor, formally canonised by Alexander III. in 1161, and Wulfstan of Worcester, similarly canonised by Innocent III. in 1203. And both these exceptions belong to the very end of the pre-Conquest period. But after Alexander III's decree no single British worthy received official honour for sanctity without papal sanction, and within a few years the most famous of English saints, St. Thomas of Canterbury, was canonised by that same pope Alexander III. Two steps still remained. The lawyer popes of the thirteenth century drew up a procedure for canonisation which, though comparatively casual and haphazard, marks a great step in advance. The beaureaucratic popes of the fourteenth century made the process of canonisation formal, juridical, rigorous and precise.

The first step towards canonisation remained as ever, public fame. This materialised into a petition to the Pope to enquire into the matter. If the Pope were convinced that a *prima facie* case were made out, he appointed a commission of enquiry ; if not convinced, he turned down the whole matter. I may say in passing that the firmness of papal action in rejecting doubtful claims, saved the English Church from a crowd of pseudo-saints and political saints of very varying merits, such as Simon de Montfort, Archbishop Winchelsea—two eminently respectable men—and Earl Thomas of Lancaster and Edward II., two eminently unworthy claimants for canonisation. A small commission of bishops, generally three in number, formed the tribunal which acted both as judge and defendant. The burden of proof was thrown upon the petitioners who were represented by procurators, counsel, as we might call them, for the prosecution. The commission sat wherever it liked; in the case of St. Thomas it sat at Naples. It heard many sworn witnesses, and carefully separated its enquiries under the two heads of life and miracles. To keep the witnesses to the point, it drew up a list of ' capitula ' or questions to which definite answers were required. All the proceedings of the commission, including the evidence, was set forth in writing by notaries. The result was the invaluable ' processus canonisationis,' records of the canonisation, which in each case of its survival gives us a full account of the saint's life and works. The process of the canonisation of St. Thomas Aquinas is peculiarly illuminating, and we owe to the testimony of his comrades, disciples, penitents and friends, first hand testimony as to the details of his life which enable us to get a clearer vision of his personality than can generally be obtained of a mediaeval worthy.

When the evidence was heard, the commissioners sent in their report to the papal curia. This was considered by the pope and cardinals, and, if approved, the saint was formally canonised by papal bull. Henceforth the honours of sanctity were due to him, though the generality of his cultus naturally varied within the sphere of his influence and the attraction of his character. His shrine became a place of pilgrimage at which wonders were expected to be wrought ; services and hymns were composed in his honour ; when his cult was well established his remains were commonly ' translated,' as was the case of St. Thomas, to a new and worthier shrine ; his name was inscribed in the calendars of saints, though in this matter a good deal was still left to local option. In the case of an early saint the extent of his cult is easily illustrated by the churches dedicated to him. A good illustration of this is St. Thomas of Canterbury, whose dedications in England far exceed those to St. Thomas the Apostle, though this is obscured to modern eyes by the rededication of the Thomas' churches to the Apostle, after Henry VIII. had unsainted the prelate who dared to oppose a king. But by the fourteenth century the great age of building churches was over. Churches were already extraordinarily numerous ; each church had its dedication already, and, if the fabric were rebuilt, the dedication remained unchanged, though sometimes, as in the case of the parish church of Manchester, its dedication was extended, on the reconsecration of the existing Cathedral under Henry V. by adding to St. Mary, the old patron saint, two new patrons of more political than religious significance, St. George of England and St. Denis of France. It follows that even the greatest of late mediaeval saints have comparatively few dedications in their honour. Even St. Francis and St. Dominic have not many ancient dedications outside the churches of their respective orders. Accordingly, the dedications to St. Thomas Aquinas are few in relation to the universality of his fame. When the growth and displacement of old popula-

tion and the extra European expansion of Christianity
to new worlds once more involved new dedications, our
saint came in for his due ; but even then modern saints
whose memory was fresher obtained the lion's share of
this particular honour.

The canonisation of St. Thomas naturally removed all
suspicion of unsoundness in his teaching. For the rest of
the Middle Ages he was not only a great example of
Christian perfection, but the wisest and profoundest
teacher as regards the whole sphere of what was then
known. When the Reformation and the Renaissance
turned their backs to the Middle Ages, and denounced
scholastic philosophy as barbarous and superstitious, there
was a strong reaction against him. But even then the
generation which abused the name of one of Thomas'
most conspicuous fellow-workers and described as a dunce
any blockhead incapable of appreciating true knowledge,
the age which denounced, in the language of Francis
Bacon, Aristotle himself as the worst of sophists, even
that age had little positive to say against the intelligence of
Thomas, however little they might dislike his methods and
his results. With the Counter-Reformation of the later
sixteenth century, Thomas got back his old credit at least
in Catholic Europe. Pius V., the most characteristic
pope of restored and revived Catholicism, saluted St.
Thomas as the fifth great doctor of the Church, and set
forth in print the whole of his voluminous works for the
edification of the faithful. This restored Thomas to his
ancient place as the most credited expounder of the faith,
until the ' enlightenment ' of the eighteenth centruy once
more assailed his fame and his wisdom. Just as after
the Reformation came the Counter-Reformation, so now
after the age of Voltaire and the Encyclopaedists came the
Romantic Revival and another Catholic Reaction. So
far as the Catholic world is concerned, this culminated in
the remarkable rehabilitation of Thomas as a philosopher
and theologian by Leo XIII., to whom scholarship owes
the last and best edition, unfortunately not yet completed,

of St. Thomas' works. Nor is this respect for Thomas limited to those of his own faith. The historical study of the Middle Ages by historians whose object is to understand rather than to uphold their point of view, has taught all serious scholars that mediaeval philosophy is no mere backwater that can be safely neglected by the student of the history of thought, but is a real link between the best thinking of antiquity and the active spirit of enquiry of modern times. We can still learn much from Aristotle, without necessarily believing in the city state, in slavery, and in the aristocratic contempt of the Greek world for the ordinary plain man. We can still learn much from Aristotle's eminent disciple, St. Thomas, and yet profoundly dissent from his religion and his philosophy. All great ages of history have their lessons for posterity, provided always that posterity is sympathetic and fair-minded. The spread of the ' scientific ' study of history has been to very little purpose if it cannot give its due to all the great men of old. And that due must not be withheld because to some of us a mediaeval, monastic, Christian, saint means a great deal more than he does to others.

St. Thomas as a Philosopher

By A. E. TAYLOR, M.A.,

Professor of Moral Philosophy in the University of St. Andrews

IF an educated Englishman had been asked a hundred years ago who are the great original philosophic thinkers of the modern world, what answer would he have been likely to give ? His list of names would, no doubt, have depended partly upon his personal preferences, but there are some philosophers whom he would have been sure to mention. He would certainly have named Descartes, Locke and Hume, and almost certainly Francis Bacon, then all the more admired because the real character of his theories in logic was so little understood. A widely read man would probably have given the names of Leibniz and Spinoza, and the few who had any knowledge of German literature would no doubt have added that of Kant. It is almost certain that no mention would have been made of St. Thomas or any of the great schoolmen of the thirteenth century. The current estimate of them is indicated by the remark made in 1828 by Macaulay that ' we extol Bacon and sneer at Aquinas.' If the same question were put to-day, there would still be individual variations in the answers, but there are some names which would be contained in them all, and I think it safe to say that among these would be that of St. Thomas. We are not to-day all of one mind in philosophy any more than our great-grandfathers were, and I do not know that it is desirable that we should be. But if we are not all of us professed Thomists, we are all, I believe, agreed to recognize in St. Thomas one of the great master-philosophers of human history whose thought is part of the permanent inheritance of civilized Europeans and whose influence is still living and salutary. It is worth while to ask ourselves what is the real ground for the great difference between our own estimate of the worth of the Thomist philosophy and that of our great-grandfathers. Their depreciation of the Angelical Doctor, however unjust, presumably had some sort of reasons for its existence, and if we can discover them, we may learn a lesson which will be profitable in saving to keep us from repeating the same kind of mistake on our own account.

To indicate some of these reasons and to point out their inadequacy will be the modest purpose of the remarks I now proceed to make.

There are two qualities which we may fairly demand from the work of any man whom we are to recognize as a really great philosopher with a permanent importance in the history of human thought. In the first place the work must be original and in the second it must be critical. When I say that the work must be original, I do not mean that it need be startling or revolutionary, but that it must be the achievement of genuine personal intellectual effort. The great philosopher must be one who has thought for himself and has thought hard. No mere skilful borrower or adapter, no mere eloquent exponent of the ideas of other men can permanently retain his place on the roll of honour of the world's great thinkers. And by saying that the work must be critical, I do not mean that it must necessarily be chiefly devoted to criticism of other men's thoughts, I mean that it must be something more than the construction of a brilliant but undisciplined speculative imagination. The great philosopher cannot, indeed, have too daring an imagination provided only that its exercise is controlled by a profound sobriety of judgment, a massive common-sense. Commonly we find the two gifts in an unequal combination. The daringly imaginative mind is apt to be deficient in sobriety of judgment, the emphatically sensible mind to be wanting in imaginative power. And perhaps, when this is the case, since the object of philosophy is the attainment of truth, the thinker of really massive common-sense, even if his imagination is slower in its flights, really does more for philosophy than the dazzling but erratic and unsystematic speculator. The greatness of St. Thomas as a philosopher seems to me to lie in this, that his work combines high originality with an unsurpassed sobriety of judgment and sense for reality. To our great-grandfathers this statement would have seemed a paradox and it is precisely because it would have struck them as a paradox that they could permit themselves, in Macaulay's phrase, to ' sneer at Aquinas.' May I attempt to state briefly what I take to have been their case ?

Thomas, I think they would have said, is not one of the world's great philosophers for the double reason that he is not original and that he is not critical. He is not original because his so-called philosophy is all borrowed and all borrowed from one man, Aristotle. And what he has taken from Aristotle is simply a frame-work of barren and verbal formal logic. He is content to treat every philosophical question as a mere matter of bringing the issue at question under the caption of some Aristotelian antithesis, like that of matter and form or potentiality and act. No doubt in effecting the reduction, he shows great skill in the construction of formal syllogisms and the multiplication of subtle verbal distinctions. But the syllogisms and distinctions do not bring us one step nearer the real understanding of concrete fact, and that is why, as was assumed, the sciences made no real advance from the thirteenth century to the seventeenth. The scholastic philosopher might devote himself as much as he pleased to the elaboration of further and further deductions from arbitrarily assumed major premisses, but so long as the premisses were not tested by confrontation with empirical fact, all this a-priorist ingenuity was worse than wasted. In the early nineteenth century view, at least, what science needs is not formal logic but guaranteed empirical fact, first, last and all the time.

And again, St. Thomas and his contemporaries are uncritical, and that in more ways than one. They are uncritical, it was held, in the first place in the selection of their great authority, Aristotle. It is an arbitrary thing to pick out this one man from among all the thinkers of the past and reject all the valuable lessons which might have been learned from other sources. It is uncritical, again, when the authority has been selected, to follow it with a blind trust in its infallibility on every subject on which it has delivered itself. And finally, it is uncritical in the highest degree to submit the conclusions of philosophical thinking to the constant overruling control of theological authority, as it was commonly assumed that St. Thomas and the other great schoolmen had done. This, I believe, is the substance of what would have been stated as the anti-scholastic case, and it must be allowed that if it could be sustained it would be enough to justify the men of a hundred years ago in their refusal to reckon seriously with the scholastic philosophies.

But the anti-scholastic case cannot really be sustained. In all that is most weighty in the indictment it rests upon complete misconception of the real situation of thought in the thirteenth century and the work which was done by St. Thomas and his teacher Albert the Great. I will deal first with the charge of want of originality and then make some remarks about the other charge of want of critical judgment. I have not, indeed, anything novel to say, but on an occasion like this, when we are assembled expressly to ' praise famous men,' it is worth while to remind ourselves of the facts which abundantly prove the real originality of Thomas.

If we are to put ourselves at the right point of view for appreciating that originality, we must begin by understanding quite clearly that the thirteenth century, like the seventeenth and the nineteenth, in their various ways, was not one of traditionalism, acquiescence in a heritage from the past, but one of restless and audacious innovation and that to the eyes of contemporaries ' Brother Thomas ' was one of the most audacious of the innovators. To speak accurately Thomism, to those who were living at the time of its birth, was not the defence of a tradition but doubly a revolt against established tradition. It is, in the first place, of course, not true that the discovery of Aristotelian

logic was the work of the thirteenth century. No doubt
scholasticism in its latest days did degenerate into something like the substitution of the mere reduction of a
problem to the technical terminology of Aristotle for the
real examination of the facts. But if we are to make this
a ground of attack against the first introducers of formal
logic into the modern Western world, the scapegoats ought
to be looked for in the twelfth and not in the thirteenth
century. It was not the latter which wasted the best of
its energies in unfruitful quarrelling about the old problem
of Universals, nor were Thomas and Albert primarily
formal logicians at all. Their Aristotle, as I need hardly
remind you, was very different from the Aristotle known
to Peter Abelard. The interest of the thirteenth century
was not in Aristotle's logical doctrines but in the teaching
of his *Metaphysics, Physics, De Caelo, De Generatione, De
Anima,* and the rest of the treatises which were recovered
for the Western world early in the century from the hands
of Jews, Persians and Moors, and the fascination of this
literature lay precisely not in its logical form but in its
matter. As M. Gilson has said, the recovery of the cos-
mological, physiological and psychological work of Aristotle
meant to the Western world the rediscovery of Nature
herself as an object of investigation in her own right and
by the ' natural light of reason.' We must recollect that
the world into which Aristotle's metaphysics and science,
as distinct from his formal logic, were reintroduced in
the early years of the thirteenth century was one which
for centuries had known only one work of real value on
what we nowadays call science,—Chalcidius's fragmen-
tary version of the *Timaeus,* and that the *Timaeus,* with
all its profound insight into the character of scientific
problems and scientific method, does not even aim at being
a repertory of scientifically ascertained conclusions of
fact. In the Aristotelian works rediscovered in the thirteenth century, Christendom was, for the first time since
the closing of the ancient Hellenic schools by Justinian,
being confronted with an encyclopædia of the Natural

Sciences as a *fait accompli* and put in a position to realise
that the external world is something more than a useful
key to the hieroglyphics of the Scriptures. There was,
indeed, to be a period, some centuries later, when a re-
kindled interest in the remains of the pre-Aristotelian
Greek thinkers would serve the same purpose of recalling
men from fancy to fact, but we misread the facts of history
if we do not realise that the enthusiasm of the thirteenth
century for Aristotle was prompted by the very same
spirit as the protests of Galileo against the Aristotelian
traditionalism of the universities of Northern Italy in the
seventeenth century. Hence M. Gilson seems absolutely
right in his contention that the return of Aristotle from
his Oriental captivity opened for scientific thought an era
not of subjection but of liberation.

This, however, is not all that has to be said about the
attitude of Thomas toward the great Greek thinkers, nor
the half of it. The next point I would raise is one on which
I have already said a passing word—the point that, whatever Thomism in some later phases may have temporarily
sunk into being, St. Thomas himself was no traditionalist
but a vigorously independent thinker who impressed his
older contemporaries as a daring innovator. In fact, as
I said, he was doubly in revolt against tradition. The
main tradition in Christian philosophical thinking, as
you all know, had right down to the days of Albert and
Thomas been the Platonic as derived through Augustine
and Boethius ; the substitution of Aristotelianism for
Platonism as the basis of a specifically Christian philosophy was a revolution and a rather paradoxical revolution.
The greatest admirer of Aristotle among you would
probably be ready to allow at least that, on the face of it,
Platonism impresses us as a deeply religious view of
existence with the closest affinities to Christianity in its
doctrines of Providence, moral judgment and retribution ;
on the face of it, again, Aristotle's thought, at first at any
rate, certainly looks to be what it has been called in recent
years by one who has a right to speak on such matters,

the least religious of the great philosophies. The task of finding a basis for a Christian philosophy precisely in the ' First Philosophy' of Aristotle was thus a singularly bold one from which any thinker without the highest intellectual independence must have flinched.

And if Thomas was thus a bold innovator on the Platonic tradition of earlier Christian thinkers, we must remember that he was equally an innovator in the interpretation he put on Aristotelianism itself. Here again there was a definite tradition confronting him, a tradition built up by men to whom, as his repeated references show, he felt that grave respect was due, Alexander of Aphrodisias, Avicenna, Averroes, Rabbi Moses, and the tradition was decidedly in favour of a pantheistic and naturalistic interpretation of Aristotle which would have been fatal to the very cause Thomas had at heart, the creation of a system of thought which was to be at once reasoned closely out at every step and wholly true to the religious demands of Christianity. The complete victory won by Thomas over the Averroists and their naturalism must not blind us to the simple fact that philosophically it was Siger of Brabant and not Thomas who was following the lines of traditional Aristotelianism. In fact, the Aristotelianism of St. Thomas triumphed over that of the Averroists not because they were *philosophically* heretics and schismatics, (they, in fact, stood for the main tradition of centuries), nor because it is demonstrably the more faithful interpretation of Aristotle's own thought,—a position on which one might argue for ever without reaching a definite conclusion—but by its sheer merits. One may convince oneself on that point very readily by a simple study of that exquisite masterpiece of philosophical polemic, the *de Unitate Intellectus contra Averroistas*. There is no pretence here that the issue at stake is decided in any way by mere exegesis of an authoritative text. The question is not what Aristotle personally meant to say, but what is true. Even if the Averroists are right in their exegesis of Aristotle, it still has to be considered whether the doctrine presented, perhaps truly, perhaps falsely, as Aristotle's is true or false. It is not concealed that the doctrine the writer of the essay believes to be true and holds to be compatible with the not very explicit utterances of Aristotle is in conflict not only with the teaching of Averroes but with the whole tradition of Aristotelian exegetes. There is no pretence that we have simply to discover what Aristotle meant and that his opinion, once ascertained, must be taken as true because it is his.

The writer's position is the very different one that it would not be at all surprising that Aristotle or any other philosopher should have fallen into an error. Our business is to satisfy ourselves by independent hard thinking, if we can, about the truth of the matter ; if we subsequently find that Aristotle's deliverances admit of being understood in a sense compatible with the truth, so much the better for him, but if they cannot be so interpreted, we have simply to say that, like everybody else, Aristotle was not infallible and has made a mistake. On the merits of the controversy it seems to me unmistakable that the Averroists receive, what is a rare thing in metaphysical controversy, a direct and crushing defeat which makes the reading of the essay a delight to anyone who can appreciate the art of ' mental warfare.' That Thomas felt this, too, I should infer from the departure at the end of the essay from his usual calm impersonality of tone. I think I detect in the sentence in which the Averroists are invited if they really have anything worth calling an argument, to produce it and see what will happen to it, an innocent chuckle, so to say, over the completeness of a triumph which the Saint evidently recognizes as due not to superior acquaintance with Aristotelian texts but to honest personal clear-headed thinking.

The plain fact, indeed,—though I am here anticipating for a moment,—is that the Aristotelianism of Thomas, if we are to call it so, is not borrowed from anyone, except in the sense in which the most original of human minds

may be said to ' borrow ' the suggestions it needs as the
pabulum for its own thinking. It is a genuinely new
systematic doctrine, indebted to Aristotle of course, and
to many others besides, but owing its specific form and
its systematic coherency to its deviser ; the right name for
it is not Aristotelianism but Thomism.

How completely the new philosophical doctrine revolu-
tionised accepted tradition in the Christian West may
perhaps be seen from two little facts doubtless familiar
to all of you.

One is the fate of the famous *a priori* argument of Anselm
for the existence of God, named by Kant the ' ontological
proof.' From the careful study of Father P. A. Daniels
it appears that out of fifteen leading schoolmen of the
thirteenth century who reproduce the argument, three, of
whom Albert the Great is one, express no opinion on its
validity, ten accept it, only two reject it, St. Thomas and
Richard of Middleton. I think we may infer that the
discredit into which the argument fell with philosophers
and theologians, to whom one would have expected it to
be specially welcome from its simplicity and apparent
finality, is wholly due to the vigour and originality of the
famous criticism to which it was subjected by Thomas.
It is highly significant that the moment Descartes attempted
to revive the same line of thought in the seventeenth
century, the critics of his *Meditations* raised the objection
that his employment of it would render his philosophy
suspect in the eyes of theologians,—the very class, as I
say, whose natural bias one would expect to be in its
favour. It is not for me, here, of course, to express any
opinion of my own on the soundness of the famous argument ; I want simply to make two observations about the
rejection of it by St. Thomas. The first is that there could
be no better proof of the independence of mind of a thinker
whose principal task in life was the philosophical defence
of religion than that he should have insisted on rigorously
criticising and rejecting the very line of argument which
promised to be the shortest of routes to Theism, and that

D

in the face of the general consensus of the *docti* in its favour. The other is that it is a point of the highest interest that there are just two great philosophers who have independently, and on different grounds, rejected the ontological argument, Thomas and Kant, and that whenever you find a philosophic thinker to-day who rejects it, you regularly find, when you come to scrutinize his ground, that he is moved directly by the considerations long ago urged by one or both of these great men. Kant and St. Thomas have often been, and still are, pitted against one another by their respective followers as natural antagonists; this makes it all the more significant that they are in complete agreement on this fundamental point, rather to the scandal of many of the so-called ' idealists ' of our own day, who would like to regard Kant as their legitimate ancestor. The secret explanation of the agreement I believe is to be found in the fact that both philosophers are really, in the best sense of the phrase, ' critical realists ' with all the realist's distrust of brilliant speculation which has no solid root in a firm grasp of empirical fact.

The other example is equally significant, and to you it will be equally familiar. Thomas seems first to have attracted attention as a thinker with an individuality of his own by his declaration that the philosophical arguments in vogue for an absolute beginning of the world's history will not stand scrutiny and that, apart from a supernatural revelation, it must remain an open question whether the created world has not existed *ab aeterno*, a position in which he agrees with Rabbi Moses. In our own day the bias of philosophers seems to be preponderantly in favour of the Aristotelian tenet of the eternity of the world, and the fact stands in the way of our appreciating the originality of this declaration at its full merits. We have to remember that the philosophical bias of the contemporaries of St. Thomas was, quite naturally, in the other direction. Since no one who was an orthodox Christian thought of doubting that the world had had a beginning at no very remote date, the tendency was naturally to attempt philo-

sophical demonstration of what was unquestionably
accepted as a known truth, and living thinkers, including
St. Thomas's own teacher Albert, had professed to be able
to supply the required proof. There is abundance of
evidence that Thomas's early declared and persistent
denial of the worth of all these demonstrations was felt
as something like a veritable scandal. It would naturally
wear that appearance all the more that the rising philosopher
would inevitably seem to be playing straight into the hands
of the ' naturalists ' of the time, the Averroists. To
appreciate the disturbance created, we have only to
remember the alarm caused to well-meaning and pious
men by the appearance of Darwin's *Origin of Species*.
We know the kind of thing which would have been said
in the middle of the nineteenth century if a rising divine
or Professor of Theology or Moral Philosophy had publicly
declared that all the arguments by which opponents of
Darwin were trying to refute the doctrine of the origination
of new species by natural selection are invalid and will not
stand examination. But to the contemporaries of St.
Thomas the assertion that there are no sound philosophical
arguments against the creation of the world ' from eternity'
involved at least as great a revolution in traditional
thinking as the doctrine of the origin of species by natural
selection demanded of our grandfathers. It could have
come from no one but a thinker of the most marked
originality and determined courage, the last kind of man
in the least likely to allow his judgment as a philosopher
to be determined for him by extra-philosophical considerations or bias in favour of a venerable tradition.

These remarks lead me naturally to the part of my
subject which happens, from the character of my own
studies, to be most interesting to myself,—the attitude of
Thomas to the philosophical thought of the world's past.
The persons for whom Macaulay is speaking in the words I
quoted at the beginning of this lecture supposed this
attitude to be sufficiently described by saying that St.
Thomas subjected human thought to the despotism of

Aristotle. But the judgment is only intelligible when we remember that the accusation dates from a time when the serious revival of Aristotelian study in Europe had barely begun. The Aristotle of the ' advanced thinkers ' of the eighteenth and early nineteenth centuries was not the Aristotle of history as we have since learned to understand him, nor even Aristotle as seen through the eyes of St. Thomas himself, but Aristotle as falsely conceived by the *epigoni* of scholasticism in its feeblest and least original period. From our point of view such an estimate ought to be at once and for all impossible. It would be truer to say that what Thomas effected for the first time in history since the expiry of neo-Platonic learning in the sixth century was a magnificent and original synthesis of past philosophical thought. He took his materials freely from the whole record of the classic past, so far as it lay open to him, and what he constructed out of them was no chaotic eclecticism but a coherent system welded into a unity by the presence throughout its details of a few great ruling principles won by permanent hard thinking and held with the clearest consciousness of their implications. It is not true that he changed the existing philosophical tradition by dethroning one uncritically accepted authority and enthroning another. It would be much truer to say that he retained and built upon the thought which had been accessible to his predecessors, enriching and integrating it with the wealth of new matter made accessible to his own age by the recovery of Aristotle. Indeed, I do not know that it would be going beyond the mark to say that, for the first time in the life of the modern world he attempted something like a critical and thoroughly historical appreciation of past philosophy in its entirety. I cannot develop this thought so fully as I should like to do, but there are certain aspects of it upon which I should like to make a few remarks.

To a student of Greek philosophy it is of great interest to note how frequent are the references in that great philosophical masterpiece, the *Summa contra Gentiles*, to the very thinkers about whom the men of the thirteenth century could have the least trustworthy information, the pre-Platonic men of science. It is curious how often the author goes out of his way to comment on the theories of men like Anaxagoras and Empedocles and what earnest efforts he makes to understand them and to call attention to the truths they may be supposed to have been struggling to convey. To be sure, many of his guesses at their meaning are such as we can now see to be unhistorical, but we have to remember the paucity of his information. In the main his knowledge about the earliest Greek thought is necessarily based on scattered notices in the text of Aristotle. He has thus to reconstruct under the double disadvantage that his knowledge is full of *lacunae* and that Aristotle's statements about his predecessors are often both obscure and vitiated by the defect, shared by Aristotle with Hegel, of inability to appreciate the ideas of others except with reference to his own system. This, however, is a difficulty common to him with all writers about the beginnings of Greek science down to a very recent date. We have to remember that the work of collating the various sources of information, correcting the often grave errors in the traditional texts and establishing the historical affiliation of the sources, an indispensable preliminary to satisfactory interpretation, can hardly have been said to have begun before the publication of Diels's *Doxographi Graeci* and the great Berlin edition of the commentators on Aristotle, well within our own life-time, and is not even yet fully completed. Bear all this in mind, and then, comparing Thomas's treatment of those of the early thinkers about whom the literature available to him contains a reasonable amount of information with Hegel's treatment of the same subject in his lectures on the *History of Philosophy*, ask yourselves which of the two men, when proper allowance is made for superiority of the material available to Hegel, has used his material in the more objective and scientific way. I honestly do not think the advantage will be found to be on the side of the German.

A more important question is that of the relation of Thomas to Plato and to Aristotle himself. Here I am afraid I shall be bound to be a little more prolix. There is a misleading but common impression that down to the middle of the thirteenth century the foundations of the philosophy of the Christian ages had been Platonic, but that at that date Thomas and Albert effected a sudden revolution by rejecting Plato for Aristotle. There is, of course, a certain truth at the bottom of this statement, but, like all summary statements, it is dangerously misleading unless it is very carefully qualified. In the first place it suggests the thoroughly unhistorical view that the philosophies of Plato and Aristotle are in principle opposed to one another, whereas the truth, as all careful students of both philosophers know, is that the differences between the two thinkers, important as some of them are, are comparatively few and are mostly on points which are quite secondary by comparison with the fundamental principles in which the two great philosophies agree. That Aristotle himself was clearly alive to this is manifest all through his work. The undisguised object of the standing polemic. which he urges against the contemporary Academy is to suggest that, in spite of all differences in formulas, in spirit it is himself and not Speusippus or Xenocrates who is the legitimate heir to the intellectual achievements of Plato. Nor do I think Plato himself would have resented this attitude. No doubt, if he could have returned to earth he would have protested that much of the Aristotelian criticism rests on misconception of his meaning, the kind of misconception inevitable when a biologist attempts to follow the thought of a mathematician. But the philosopher who deliberately refused to compose a treatise on his own philosophy on the ground that philosophy is not a body of formulae or doctrines, but the living spirit of personal devotion to the pursuit of truth, would have been the last man to disown a successor on the strength of a difference in expression or opinion.

The popular conception again completely misrepresents

the facts about the actual achievement of Thomas. It is true that on a first perusal of him we are struck by the uniformity with which the familiar Aristotelian technical formulae recur in his treatment of all questions. His logical equipment, in particular, comes direct from the *Topics* and the *Analytics*. This is, in any case, what we should expect. There was, in fact, no other body of articulated logical doctrine with which to work. But when we penetrate to the matter which is presented to us in this vesture of Aristotelian logic, the case is altered. The Augustinian exemplarism, itself a direct derivation of the Platonic doctrine of Forms, is, as we know, an important and integral part of the Thomist philosophy. Intimately connected with it is the equally fundamental conception of causality as a process in which the effect imperfectly ' mirrors ' the cause, and this, with the great notion of the ladder of being, or scale of perfection, is wholly a legacy, through Augustine, from the neo-Platonists. It is, I think, safe to say that none of these conceptions could have been derived from the text of Aristotle unless Aristotle had first been read by the light of Platonism and neo-Platonism as mediated through Augustine.

Indeed, I should like to go rather further than this. It seems to me at least an ambiguous statement to say that Thomas directly opposes Platonism in metaphysics at all. He certainly opposes particular doctrines of the *Platonici*, but it is another question whether he can be said to oppose the doctrines of Plato. (I am speaking, of course, of the Platonic metaphysic ; I do not refer to psychology and the theory of knowledge, where we all know that Thomism is definitely Aristotelian). Before we can say that Thomas opposes the Platonism of Plato, we need to be quite sure what Plato's own ripest thought was, and to be sure on that point is a very difficult matter. The trouble is that Plato has himself been at some pains to warn us that his deepest thoughts are not to be found in his writings ; he reserved them, in fact, for oral exposition to the students of the Academy. Our knowledge of them has to be gathered in the first instance from the allusions of Aristotle, who notoriously treats as the distinctive doctrines of Plato propositions which are not to be found in the Platonic dialogues at all. Unfortunately Aristotle is most commonly content to make enigmatic statements without explaining what they mean, a task which would be superfluous while the original hearers of Plato were alive and active, and even when he gives an explanation we cannot be sure that it is one which Plato himself would have accepted as accurate. The dramatist's gift of entering with ready sympathy into the inmost thought of another mind appears, indeed, to have been one with which Aristotle, with all his other gifts, was not richly endowed. The indispensable preliminary to real comprehension of Plato's personal thought would seem to be a careful collection of all the notices of his oral teaching to be found in Aristotle and a confrontation of them with all the similar records of such notices by Xenocrates and other Academics as still survive in the commentaries of Simplicius and other men of learning in later antiquity. This preliminary work has only been systematically undertaken within the present century by the industry of M. Robin,[1] and the task of interpreting the material he has collected for us cannot be said to have advanced beyond its bare inception. It will be time to raise the question whether Thomism and Platonism are really in fundamental antagonism when we have rediscovered, if we ever do rediscover it, the real tradition of the first generation of the Academy. Meanwhile, I may perhaps be allowed to utter a word or two by way of caution. If, as seems perhaps probable, Plato really meant to make the world of Forms which is the object of science something existing apart from God, independent of Him and above Him in the scale of perfection, it need not be said that Thomas completely rejects that part of his teaching, though the rejection is not a conscious repudiation of Plato, since no one in the thir-

[1] L. Robin, *la Théorie Platonicien des Idées et des Nombres d'après Aristote*. Paris, 1908.

teenth century understood Plato in this sense.   So far as I
have observed in my own reading, what polemic there is
against the *Platonici* in the principal works of St.   Thomas
is principally connected with two points, (1) that Plato
regards ' natural species ' as substances and (2) that the
' *Platonici* ' have said that the soul is in the body as the
sailor is in his ship.   The first of these statements about
Plato is certainly borne out by well-known polemical
passages in Aristotle, though it is interesting to remember
that the precise meaning and the justification of these
Aristotelian criticisms is still hotly controverted among
special students of Greek philosophy.   The second statement seems to an outsider like myself a little of a puzzle.
The phrase about the sailor and the vessel does not actually
occur anywhere in Plato and is not really well-chosen to
illustrate the view about the relation between the soul and
the body suggested even in the *Phaedo*.   St. Thomas
presumably took the phrase from the passage in the *de
Anima* where Aristotle says that the problem is one which
will have to be considered.   The curious thing is that the
ancient commentators were all completely in the dark
about the bearings of the observation ;   they are quite
uncertain whose theory is alluded to, and even uncertain
whether Aristotle meant to express approval or disapproval.
The one thing they do not suggest is that the reference is
to Plato.   Possibly, then, St. Thomas was mistaken in
seeing any reference to Plato in the words.   In any case
the real attitude of Thomas to the great thinker who had
inspired the philosophical thought of Augustinianism
cannot be properly determined by reference to this rather
special and limited polemic.   It is much more significant,
though it is too often forgotten, that Thomism incorporates
in itself the whole of the Augustinian exemplarism.   This
really brings Thomas much nearer to Plato than Aristotle
himself is, at least in his controversial moods.   Aristotle
often allows himself to speak as though the whole Platonic
doctrine of Forms or Ideas had been ' moonshine,' ' empty
words ' ; Thomas never says anything of the kind.   In

his theory the archetypal Forms have an important part
to play ; it is only that Plato was mistaken in supposing
that they are directly accessible to *our* imprisoned intelligence.

And what of the relation of Thomas to Aristotle himself ?
Is not this equally misrepresented when he is spoken of as
an ' Aristotelian ' or a ' follower of Aristotle ' without
further explanation ?   Clearly I think in using such un-
qualified expressions there is the danger of creating a
thoroughly false impression.   There is one sense in which
Thomas is no follower of Aristotle nor of any other man.
He never accepts a doctrine because it has been taught by
a man with a famous name and an established reputation ;
what he accepts he accepts because he believes it to be
true, or if not absolutely and certainly true, the nearest
approximation that can be made to the exact truth.   If
then he, in many parts of his philosophizing, follows
Aristotle so closely, it is because he is convinced by the
independent exercise of his personal thinking powers that
Aristotle is on the right lines.   You will remember how
explicitly this point is made in the annihilating critique
of the Averroist doctrine about the ' unity of the intellect.'
We are told there, as plainly as we could be told, that our
real concern is not with what Aristotle taught but with
what is true.   If the Averroists could succeed in showing
that their own exegesis of Aristotle is correct, that would
be so much the worse for Aristotle, but none the better
for Averroes.   The sanction of Aristotle is never an
adequate refuge for error.   One remembers, too, how
in the commentary on the *de Caelo* we are explicitly warned
against the very mistake made by the traditionalists of
the time of Galileo.   We may be content, we are told, to
accept the scheme of the Aristotelian (or rather Eudoxian)
astronomy, because ' it saves the appearances,' but we
must not insist that the machinery it assumes of the rotat-
ing spheres is real, ' because it is quite possible that the
appearances may equally well be saved by some other
theory yet to be put forward.'   That is, in modern language,

we may use the current astronomy as a convenient des-
criptive theory on the strength of which eclipses and other
astronomical events may be correctly calculated, but we
have no right to treat the description as if it were an
explanation. It is plain, I think, that if Thomas, who was,
of course, well acquainted with the fact that a heliocentric
astronomy had been taught in antiquity by Aristarchus
and Seleucus, could have been confronted with the revival
of the theory by Copernicus, he at least would have been
ready to consider with an absolutely open mind the
question whether the heliocentric theory does not 'save
the appearances' better than the geocentric.

In general, as to this matter of the degree of dependence
of St. Thomas on Aristotle, there are, it seems to me, one
or two things well worth saying even in a brief paper like
this. (1) I suppose no one has ever made an extensive
and repeated study of the *Corpus Aristotelicum* without
feeling strongly that there were, so to say, two Aristotles.
There was the Aristotle whose tendencies are to
'naturalism' in philosophy and to detailed and specific
research in the sciences, and there was the Aristotle who
was 'carried off his feet,' as Professor Burnet has said,
in the Academy by the Platonic passion for the divine
and eternal. The consequence of this manifest clash in
the philosopher's own soul between the 'naturalistic'
bent, presumably acquired in early education, and the
'otherworld' tendency due to Platonism is a curious
'fault' which runs through all the chief Aristotelian
treatises. Thus, just by way of indicating the presence
of the 'fault,' let me suggest the questions (*a*) what is,
according to Aristotle, the proper specific object of 'first
philosophy'? Is it 'being as such,' or is it the eternal
and absolute being, the 'unmoved first mover'? (*b*) Is
it really possible to fit on the few broken and enigmatic
remarks of the *de Anima* about the imperishable 'active
intellect' to the general straightforward naturalistic
account of the process of knowing and its presuppositions?
Does not one feel of all the exegeses alike, 'this may be, in

point of fact. what Aristotle ought to have said, but I cannot convince myself that it is what he actually meant to say ? ' (c) Or again, does any of us believe that Aristotle has really succeeded in his *Ethics* in harmonizing the view that the good for man is the special object of the science of ' Politics,' and thus belongs altogether to the ' active life,' with the other view which he springs on us at the end of his argument that our truest good can only be found in ' contemplation ' ?

On the face of things, Aristotle's philosophy as Aristotle himself left it, is an imperfectly achieved attempt to hold together a secular or ' one-world ' and a religious or ' two-world ' view of things. The ordinary ' naturalist ' is content to see only the one world of the sensible and present ; the ' Platonist ' is so interested in the ' other ' world of the unseen and eternal that his tendency is to come as near as he dares to treating ' this ' present world as a shadow or a bad dream. For a thoroughly critical philosophy the problem is precisely how to combine aright the two complementary attitudes of frank acceptance of the ' secular present ' and the noble ' detachment ' which refuses to accept it for more than it is worth. In Aristotle's own philosophy, as it seems to me, both attitudes find their recognition, but they are not harmonized ; they simply alternate. The general rule is that in any considerable work of Aristotle you start with what seems to be a thorough-going ' empirical ' ' secular ' or ' this-world ' attitude to the world and an avowed opposition to everything that is ' transcendental.' But by the time you reach the end of the treatise, you find yourself landed in the full-blown ' transcendental,'—' the unmoved mover,' the ' imperishable active intellect,' ' the contemplative life,' without any clear indication of the way in which the transition has been effected. Here, as it seems to me, the so-called Aristotelianism of Thomas is much more thoroughly thought out and coherent than what I may call the Aristotelianism of Aristotle. The ' this-worldly ' and the ' other-worldly ' are not juxtaposed ; the one is subordinated to the other in virtue of definite guiding principles clearly laid down and the relations of the superior to the subordinate are made logically transparent. To my own mind the clarity which is thus brought into the treatment of this supreme problem of the relation of the eternal and the secular is the best proof of all of the genuine originality of the Thomistic thought and of its perennial significance for all generations of men. I may give as an instance of the quality I have in mind the treatment of the relation of the temporal and eternal good of man in the third book of the *Summa contra Gentiles*, as compared with the treatment of the relation between the life of practice and the life of speculation in the *Nicomachean Ethics*. I do not think there can be much doubt here which of the two philosophers show the coherency, lucidity and assurance which mark the utterance of one who is really master of his theme.

For my immediate purpose, which is to urge that the Thomist philosophy is no mere Aristotelianism revised but a masterly synthesis of both Plato and Aristotle with one another and with Augustine, effected by original insight of the first order, it is particularly important to make two remarks.

As I have said, in the thought of Aristotle himself, when one tries to study it in a strictly historical spirit without preconceptions, there appear to be two conflicting strains, the naturalistic or positivist and the Platonist. Hitherto students have been content to note the fact without attempting to discuss the question of the historical development of Aristotle's own mind. From the rise of the succession of expert Aristotelian exegetes in the first century of our era down to the dawn of our own twentieth century, the encyclopaedic ' work ' of the great thinker has only too successfully hidden his personality from us. The first serious systematic attempt known to me to reconstitute the features of the son of Nicomachus as a living personality with a history of growth behind it, has only just been made by Werner Jaeger in his fascinating

Aristoteles, published only last year.[1] Many of Jaeger's special results must, no doubt, be considered tentative and I have elsewhere tried to show that in some cases he has fallen into definite errors. But in the main I feel confident that he has made out his principal thesis, and that we can distinguish in all the principal works of Aristotle well-marked earlier and later sections, the general formula being that Aristotle starts on his personal career as a convinced and enthusiastic Platonist, passes through a phase in which he attempts to show that all that is most fundamental in the ' other-worldly ' Platonic metaphysic and ethics can still be retained when the doctrine of ' Separate Forms ' has been eliminated, and ends by approximating more and more closely to the cultivation of an almost purely empirical and positivist cultivation of the details of the special sciences. If this is so, I think we may safely say that it is Aristotle the Platonist rather than Aristotle the positivist who influences the thought of Thomas.

To illustrate by one or two examples. Jaeger has, I think, made it clear that there is a shift in the *Metaphysics* as it stands from the conception of ' first philosophy ' as the study of ' being supreme and eternal ' to the thought of it simply as the study of ' being as such,' and the only reasonable explanation of the shift is that the parts of the work where the conception of ' theology ' as the crown of science is dominant come from manuscripts of the transition period, in which Aristotle is still concerned with the exposition of a real though remodelled Platonism, those in which ' first philosophy ' is equated with the science of ' being as such ' from those of the later and more positivist period. So with special reference to the famous book of the *Metaphysics* which expounds the conception of God as the ' unmoved first mover,' I cannot resist the arguments used by Jaeger to prove that in the main we are dealing with Aristotle in his earlier vein, while the chapter which introduces the fifty odd ' unmoved movers ' of the

[1] Jaeger, *Aristoteles*. Berlin, 1923.

planetary spheres is a later addition in the interests of
positive science, but wholly out of keeping with the tone
of its context.   As Jaeger says, from the point of view of
this addition, God sinks from the position of being the one
supreme and abiding source of all temporality to the
position of something like a mere unknown cause of the
diurnal revolution of the heavens, an astronomical hy-
pothesis much on the same level as gravitational attraction
in the *Principia* of Newton, or, if you prefer it, of the as
yet undiscovered cause of gravitation of which Newton
speaks in the concluding *Scholium Generale.*

Now there cannot be the slightest doubt that it is
Aristotle in what seems to be his earlier vein, the Platonist
Aristotle, who means so much to Thomas.   One may doubt
whether if the *Metaphysics* had been completely worked
over from the point of view of the chapter on the planetary
movers, so that God appeared throughout simply as the
first member of a whole series of unknown causes of movements of rotation, the book would have had much fascination for him.   Or I may make the same point in another
way.   I have sometimes asked myself what are, when all
is said, the two or three leading conceptions drawn from
Aristotle which are all-pervasive in the system of Thomas.
I believe, though I am of course offering only my own
personal impression, that we may reduce the list, if we
confine ourselves to matters of absolutely first-rate importance, to two.   One is the great conception of ' potentiality'
and the significance for every branch of science of the
distinction between potentiality and act.   I know that in
modern times there has been a violent revolt against this
distinction and that many philosophies have made determined attempts to get rid of the notion of potentiality
once and for all and to recognize nothing but actuality.
The revolt was primarily intelligible and in many respects
salutary.   I take it, it would be generally admitted that
there is some foundation for Francis Bacon's complaint
that Aristotle and his followers had corrupted natural
science by this *frigida distinctio.*   The schoolmen of the

decadence really did tend to forget that the distinction
never affords a sufficient description, not to say an explanation, of the specific detail of any process in nature, and for
my own part I think to some extent they could plead the
unfortunate example of Aristotle himself for their error.
Since no philosopher is infallible, I should not be much
surprised if Thomas himself can be proved to be sometimes
a sinner in this way.   But the history of biology or
psychology, or any science which deals with objects which
live and grow on characteristic lines, is enough to prove
that in philosophy to ignore potentiality and treat the
not yet actual as simply ' what is not ' leads to nothing but
confusion and disaster.   Insistance on the conception of
the ' potential ' seems to me to be one of the most valuable
features of the intellectual inheritance which we have to
thank the great men of the thirteenth century for pre-
serving for us.   The other great fundamental principle
which strikes me as all-important is the famous doctrine
of the equivocity of ' being ' (or, if you like to put the point
differently, of the irreducibility of the categories to any
one supreme category), which is perhaps even more
important for Thomism than for Aristotle himself, since
it is the foundation of the whole theory of analogical
knowledge as the means of escape from sheer ignorance
of the supra-temporal in philosophy.   It happened that
some time ago I was reading simultaneously Eriugena's
famous *de divisione naturae* and the *Summa contra Gentiles*,
and naturally found myself led to make some comparisons.
On one point, to be frank, I had to confess that Eriugena
seemed to me to have an advantage ; whatever one might
think of his conclusions, one could not but be impressed
by the extraordinary vigour of a speculative imagination
to which one seemed to find no later parallel until one came
down to Giordano Bruno in the full tide of the anti-
scholastic reaction.   Yet, on the other hand, quite apart
from any consideration of theological consequences, one
could not help feeling that, regarded simply as philosophical speculations, the speculations of Eriugena, like

those of Bruno after him, were undisciplined and fanciful ;
one was dealing with the work of an imagination hardly
controlled by sober judgment.   The question this reflection
suggested to me, as I thought by contrast of the magnificent
sobriety of Thomas, was this.   Was there any fundamental
philosophical principle, unknown to John the Scot, which
served to keep the thirteenth-century thinkers secure from
the excesses of an unregulated imagination ?   If there was,
was it a principle which they derived from their study of
Aristotle and could not equally well have learned from
Plato and the Platonists, who were as well known to a
learned man in the ninth century as to the learned in the
thirteenth ?   My own answer was that, so far as I could
see, the principle wanted, a principle which could not well
have been thoroughly learned except from Aristotle, was
precisely this principle that ' being is predicated equi-
vocally ' or, in other words, that the categories form an
irreducible plurality.   This, as it seems to me, is the
ultimate principle on which all the wild and dangerous
philosophical Monisms must be shipwrecked, the safeguard of sane and sober critical thinking, the one indes-
pensable form of ' pluralism ' which must reappear in any
philosophy with pretensions to be true.

Now both these principles belong as much to the earlier
Aristotle as to the later.   The distinction between potentiality and act, though best known to us from the promi-
nence given to it in Aristotelianism, appears to have
originated in the Platonic Academy and to have been the
common property of the school.   The immediate proof of
this is that we find the distinction already employed without explanation, as something familiar, in a fragment of
Aristotle's lost *Protrepticus* which must have been written
before the death of Plato, and can be seen from the remains
preserved from it by later writers to have been an eloquent
exposition of Platonism.   Indeed we may fairly go a step
further back.   In the famous passage of the *Theaetetus*
where Plato is making the distinction between knowledge
in actual use and knowledge which we have acquired and

E

can revive on occasion but are not actually using (*Tht.*
197 c.) we have the very phrase that ' in a sense we have
none of these pieces of knowledge, when we are not using
them,' what we have is the 'power' of putting our hand on
them. It is, I think, not unlikely that this observation
is the starting point of the whole doctrine of potentiality
and act, though, if it is, this of course in no way lessens
our debt to Aristotle for his recognition of the fundamental
importance of the distinction and its significance for the
whole study of nature and of man.

The other great principle of the irreducibility of the
categories is nowhere, so far as I know, touched on in
Plato, and I do not feel sure that the later world would
have arrived at it without great difficulty if it had not been
able to learn the lesson from Aristotle. At the same time,
it is fully in accord with the principles of Plato. Even of
Xenocrates, against whom in particular, the majority of
Aristotle's attacks on the Academy appear to have been
aimed, we happen to know that he contented himself with
the reduction of the categories to two, Substance and
Relation. We may say then, I believe, that if the
Thomistic metaphysics may be called Aristotelian in the
sense that it is to Aristotle they are directly indebted for
their most fundamental formulae, it is a misapprehension
to regard them as Aristotelian in the sense that they are in
principle anti-Platonic. They represent rather a rich and
full synthesis and co-ordination into a systematic whole
of the results won by the thousand years' long travail
of Greek philosophical thought, a synthesis only possible
to a mind of the first order. It has been said that Kant,
by far the most epoch-making of modern philosophers,
aims at a synthesis of Hume and Leibniz as imperfectly
apprehended through Wolff. The remark was not, of
course, meant as a disparagement of Kant's originality;
the suggestion is that the very achievement of such a
synthesis is itself only possible to a thinker of the
most absolute originality. But, by comparison with the
Thomist synthesis of Plato, Aristotle and Augustine, how

comparatively incoherent and loose is Kant's synthesis of Hume and Leibniz. The one has the unity of a great work of art, the other is by comparison an ill-constructed amalgam which visibly falls to pieces under the reader's eyes.

In epistemology and psychology the case stands rather differently. Here the foundations of the Thomist edifice may really be called Aristotelian in the more special sense which I have just deprecated for the Thomistic metaphysics. And I confess that it is just here that my own difficulties about what seems to be St. Thomas' teaching begin. I find it for example—perhaps the fault lies simply with my own failure to understand—hard to reconcile the character of our knowledge in pure mathematics with the restriction of the functions of the intellect in man to the work of abstraction from what is given in sense, and again to satisfy myself that the theory of the part played by the 'sensible species' in perception is quite consistent with itself and with the surely sound conviction that the perceived qualities of things are real qualities of real things and not 'psychical additions' to the reality. And yet, for all my difficulties, here again I feel convinced that if we would make progress to a sound theory, we cannot do better than go to school to St. Thomas. It is a striking sign of the times that contemporary philosophy is coming more and more to busy itself with precisely the problems which confront us in the Thomist epistemology and psychology of knowledge. The tendency is certainly spontaneous, since most of those who exhibit it in a very marked degree are pretty obviously quite unacquainted with all mediaeval philosophy. Yet it is undeniable that something like a return to the mental outlook of the thirteenth century is being forced upon us to-day in at least two ways. We have witnessed a widespread and vigorous revolt against the type of epistemological theory —ultimately derivable from Kant—which attempts to safeguard scientific knowledge against sceptical criticism by pronouncing the scientific character of that knowledge, its universality and necessity, to be a 'psychic addition' put into things by the human mind *de suo*. If we choose to define the very ambiguous word 'Idealism' arbitrarily as meaning the doctrine that universality and necessity are 'put into nature by the knowing mind,' we may fairly say that there are no 'idealists,' in this sense, left to-day. The epistemologist of to-day, as compared with his predecessors of forty years or more since, usually has the advantage of superior knowledge of some specific branch of science, and the influence of science, both natural and mathematical, is shown in this widespread conviction that a true theory of knowledge must treat knowing of all kinds from the outset not as a process of 'creating' but as an adventure of discovery. We do not put 'the categories' into Nature ; we find them there. This view of the relation between the knowing mind and the Nature it knows of itself takes us back to the 'critical Realism' characteristic of the philosophy of an age earlier than the unfortunate subjectivisation of the philosophical problem by Descartes.

It is significant, also that, as the current literature shows, the reaction towards what I may call an epistemological realism has once more made actual a whole class of problems prominent in Thomistic philosophy but until recently too lightly dismissed by most later thinkers. When we have convinced ourselves that the apprehension of Nature is not, as Descartes too long led us to believe, indirect, through the mediation of 'ideas,' but direct and first-hand, so that we immediately perceive the genuine qualities of real things, we are confronted, of course, with the difficult task of correctly explaining the facts which have been the stronghold of the theory of indirect or representative perception (facts about double vision, hallucinations, dreams, etc.), and of devising a really sound scientific account of the function of the processes which *in the organism*, though not in the mind's apprehension, intervene between stimulation of the sense-organ and awareness of the apprehended quality. In a word we have back on our hands precisely the same questions. which in the philosophy of Thomas are answered by the theory of the sensible and the intelligible ' species.' As I have confessed, I have never been able to feel sure that I quite grasp St. Thomas's thought on this subject, though I do seem to discern that it is much subtler than the rather crude psychology apparently intended by Aristotle himself. But this at least is clear, that a theory of perception and perceptual knowledge which is to meet the acquirements of modern science will have to be something in its general character very much like that of Thomas.   It will have to combine, as he at any rate meant to combine, the two complementary positions that our knowledge of the world around our bodies is mediated in fact by highly complicated processes of a very special kind, and that *as knowledge* it is *direct, unmediated* apprehension not of ' ideas ' or ' images ' but of actual physical reality.   No one, so far as I know, among the great modern philosophers has ever seen as clearly as Thomas that the problem is precisely not to sacrifice one of these true positions to the other.   Hence we may fairly say that the great task awaiting the epistemologist at this moment is no other than the task of providing us with an equivalent, expressed in terms of all that we know about the physiology of the brain and sense-organs, for the Thomistic doctrine of the part played in perception and perceptual knowledge by the sensible and intelligible ' species.'   For all I know, it is possible that the theory as it stands only needs to be translated into the language of modern physiological psychology, without further modification, to prove the very truth of which the epistemology of the present moment is so anxiously in search. Even if it should not be so, and modification as well as translation is called for, I am at least sure that the careful study of the Thomist doctrine on the subject is the best preparation for fruitful meditation of one's own, and that the bad habit of beginning the study of so-called ' modern ' philosophy with Descartes, in whom the epistemological problem is falsified from the first by ' representationist ' assumptions, is responsible for generations of mere fumbling in the dark which might have been escaped if the gentlemen of the eighteenth and nineteenth centuries had been willing to do less ' sneering at Aquinas ' and more study of him.

The Theology of St. Thomas

By ÆLRED WHITACRE, O.P., S.T., PRÆS.

I

Faith and Reason

PHILOSOPHY is the love of wisdom. Properly speaking, to philosophise is the occupation of the wise-man. Now the wise-man is the personification of Order, for it is he who knows how to order things well as it behoves, and to regulate them in view of their end.[1] First of all the wise-man regulates or orders the acts of his reason, for he judges and reasons well. He then strives to acquire a knowledge of, and to understand, the order among things outside himself, things that are independent of him. In the measure that he attains this knowledge he is able to regulate or order things that depend upon him as an individual, as a member or head of a family, or as a member of a state.

Now there is a wisdom in every art or craft and science. For if things are to be well ordered or regulated, it is that they might be the better disposed towards the attainment of their end, which is their good. Hence the man who uses and disposes of things in the best way, according to the end for which they were made, is said to be wise in this or that particular branch of art or learning.

But, absolutely speaking, the name of wise-man is reserved to him alone whose occupation consists not in the consideration of the end of any one particular thing, but in the consideration of the end of the whole universe. Wherefore St. Thomas,[2] quoting Aristotle,[3] says that the occupation of the wise-man or the philosopher is the consideration of the highest causes.

[1] *Topic*. Lib. II., Cap. 1, and *Metaph*. Lib. I., Cap. 2.
[2] *Cont. Gent*. Lib. I., Cap. 1.   [3] *Metaph*. Lib. I., Cap. 2.

Now what is the first cause or last end of the Universe ? The last end of any one thing is that which is intended by its author or mover when he made it. But the first cause or mover of the universe is mind, as is proved by St. Thomas in the *Contra Gentes*, Lib. II., Cap. 23 and 24.

It follows, therefore, that the last end of the universe is the good of mind ; and this is truth. The ultimate end then of the whole universe must be truth, the contemplation of which is the principal object of wisdom.

Now following in the footsteps of Aristotle,[1] St. Thomas [2] shows that the first philosophy or metaphysics is the knowledge not of any kind of truth, but of that truth which is the origin of all truth ; this first truth from which all other truth is derived is called God.

Hence it is that the supreme object of the study of philosophy is God. All departments of philosophy are so many stepping-stones to the final treatise of metaphysics, which treats not of the ultimate causes or reasons of any one thing in particular but of the most abstract notions that are transcendental to all things without exception, namely of *being* as such and its properties. It must not, however, be thought that the final aim of metaphysics is the contemplation of being as being and of its first causes. Metaphysical speculation ascends far beyond an examination of being in general, for it seeks to know and to contemplate the first and final cause of all being.[3] For this reason, St. Thomas leaves aside the consideration of being as such, and defines metaphysics by the supreme object of its contemplation, namely the first principle of being which is God ; the sufficient reason and ultimate explanation of all being is the plenitude of being or *Actus Purus*, *viz.* God. Hence the final goal of the philosopher is a knowledge of the Supreme Being, the contemplation of which is the apotheosis of wisdom.

For this reason St. Thomas says,[4] of all pursuits in the world among men, the study of wisdom is the most perfect,

---

[1] *Metaph*. Lib. I., Cap. 2.
[3] *Cont. Gent*. Lib. I., Cap. 1.
[2] *Cont. Gent*. Lib. I., Cap. 1.
[4] *Ibid*., Cap. 2.

the most sublime, the most useful and the most delightful ; for ' her conversation hath no bitterness, nor her company any tediousness, but joy and gladness.' [*Wisdom* viii. 16.]

Theology also is a wisdom which consists in the contemplation of God. The seventh article of the first question in the *Summa Theologica* proves this.[1] Is there then any difference between the philosopher and the theologian ? There is the greatest difference, and the difference is of prime importance. The theologian attains to a far greater and far more perfect knowledge of God than the philosopher. The reason is because the philosopher has only one medium of reaching God, whereas the theologian has two. The philosopher uses the natural light of his reason ; the theologian uses both the light of reason and revelation.

Let us examine these two ways of attaining a knowledge of the Supreme Being, and we shall see their difference, their merit, and, if any, their point of contact.

First of all there is the natural power of reason ; by its light a certain knowledge of God can be acquired. But the question is to find out whether our reason is sufficient for learning the Divine truths. Natural reason, by its own power, most certainly permits us to acquire certain truths relative to God and His nature. Philosophers are able to establish by demonstration that God exists, that He is one, that He is good, etc. It is, however, manifest that there is a knowledge of the Divine nature which absolutely exceeds the reach of human reason. Indeed St. Thomas proves in the very first article of the *Summa* the fittingness of a science other than philosophy precisely on this account. This article shows in how great a degree those philosophers err who consider all affirmations concerning God as false which cannot be established by reason. All the arguments that prove the existence of such a body of truths are founded upon the fact of the disproportion that exists between our mind and the Divine essence.[2] We take it then for granted, here, that there are truths concerning

---

[1] Utrum Deus sit subjectum hujus scientiæ.   [2] *Cont. Gent.* Lib. I., Cap. 3

God which are accessible to reason, and others that are inaccessible.

If we were all philosophers, philosophy would suffice to teach us all we could know of God naturally as the author of nature; but it would teach us nothing of the supernatural God. Seeing therefore we are destined to a supernatural end, then philosophy is not sufficient; there is necessary another science which is called theology.

But apart from this, even as regards a knowledge of God through reason, since all people are not philosophers, it is fitting that even those truths of God that can be attained by natural reason should be revealed, otherwise few would ever have a knowledge of God at all. Absolutely speaking, wherever reason has its full play and can attain to the knowledge of a truth by its own powers, faith has nought to do, for such a truth absolutely speaking is outside its province. In other words it is impossible that of one and the same truth there should be both faith and scientific knowledge.[1] The object of faith is that precisely which reason cannot attain; from which it follows that all reasoned knowledge which is founded on the first principles of reason is shut off from the domain of faith.

This, of course, is the consideration of the question *de jure*, but *de facto* faith has to be substituted for reason in many cases, not merely because many truths are believed by the ignorant that are known scientifically by the learned, but because it often happens through the defect of reasoning power that much error is mixed up with the conclusions that we draw. Many cannot see the probative force of an argument and consequently can have no certain knowledge of truths that are demonstrated. Further, the disagreement even among the learned on certain important points leaves the mind in doubt. It is therefore most useful and salutary that the Divine clemency should reveal, and make articles of faith the truths attainable by reason, so that all might have the benefit of this knowledge of God easily without fear of error and from the beginning of their lives.

---

[1] *De Verit.* Q. XIV., a. 9, and *Summa* IIa, IIae, Q. I., a. 5.

On the other hand, taking for granted there are truths of God beyond the reach of reason, it is evident that if we are to know them at all they must be revealed. Now it is also evident that the human race must have a certain knowledge of these truths from the fact that the human race is destined to a supernatural end.

It must know the end for which it is striving, and this knowledge can never be attained by reason, because if so the end would cease to be supernatural. The first article in the *Summa* is then justified—other than philosophy there is necessary another science called theology, which argues its conclusions from articles of faith which are its principles, just as philosophy argues its conclusions from the first principles of reason.[1]

Now it cannot be said that faith is in conflict with reason. Far from being opposed to reason, faith confers on reason its full perfection. Indeed we cannot know anything of God unless we come to see that He is above and beyond all that human thought can reach. But it is evident that to ask reason to accept truths concerning God that are inaccessible to reason is the most sure means of bringing us to a knowledge of God's incomprehensibility.[2] Further, faith suppresses presumption, which is the cause of much error. There are, indeed, some who try to measure the incomprehensibility of God by the measure of their reason ; it is useful for such as these to learn in the name of divine authority that there are truths beyond the reach of their reason. Thus does faith benefit reason.

In the *Contra Gentes* St. Thomas is at great pains to show that faith does not conflict with reason because truth cannot be opposed to truth. The truths of the Christian faith are beyond the reach of reason, but they are not contrary to it. The very first principles whereby reason works are most evidently true, so that it is not possible for reason even to think they are false ; in like manner it is impossible for the mind that holds truths by faith to think they are false since they are confirmed by signs that

[1] *Summa* I., Q. I., a. 8.   [2] *Cont. Gent.* Lib. I., Cap. 5.

are divine. Hence error only is contrary to the true, as is manifest from their very definitions, and it is impossible by the very principles whereby reason naturally works that the truths of faith should be contrary to them. Since God is the author of our nature, it follows that the first principles whereby reason works are a part of the Divine wisdom. Whatever then is contrary to these principles is contrary to the Divine wisdom. It is impossible, therefore, that what is held by faith through divine revelation should be contrary to our reasoned knowledge.

Truth is the common object both of faith and reason; they differ only in their method. The knowledge that the earth is round is acquired by at least two methods, one of which is proper to astronomy and the other proper to physics. Astronomy and physics do not differ as regards the roundness of the earth, but only as regards their method of acquiring this conclusion. It may be that astronomy is able to draw more conclusions by its own proper method, such as physics is incapable of deducing by its own method. If this is so it cannot be said that astronomy is opposed to physics, but that it is a science capable of reaching conclusions beyond the reach of physics. In like manner faith does not differ from reason except by its method of acquiring a truth. One and the same truth may be held by the mind, whether the mind attain that truth by its own proper method of reasoning or by the method of credible authority. If, however, faith through its own proper method arrives at the knowledge of truths that the light of reason cannot see, it cannot be said that faith is opposed to reason, but that owing to its peculiar method faith reaches truths that are beyond the scope of the method used by reason.

Let us now examine the points of contact between faith and reason, and we shall see that between them there is a mutual influence : just as grace perfects nature, so does faith perfect reason and give to it the means of a greater development ; on the other hand reason can help faith, for in a very strict sense reason is its handmaid.

The transcendent influence of faith upon reason is a most important point to establish in the theology of St. Thomas. Many have founded their criticisms of theology upon the pretended fact that in theology there is a mixing up of faith and reason. Now far from mixing up faith and reason, and confounding their entirely different spheres of activity, St. Thomas confines each within its own proper province, and yet brings them into closest contact without ever once confounding them together. It is indeed this that makes for the admirable unity of his philosophic and theologic speculations. One cannot read St. Thomas for long without coming to the conviction that the vast system of the world he presents to our eyes, depends upon the measure in which he leans upon faith for his guide. For St. Thomas the salutary guide of reason is faith.

At first sight one might think that in the realm of theology there is no place at all for philosophic speculation, especially if it be a question of truths entirely beyond the reach of reason. It is evident reason cannot comprehend such truths, least of all demonstrate them ; but, knowing through the higher knowledge of faith that there are here hidden truths, the mind is able by judicious comparison and argumentation to perceive things that otherwise it would never perceive.

We have seen that faith and reason do not contradict each other ; if however, on the other hand, it is certain that reason cannot demonstrate the revealed truths, it is no less certain that all so-called demonstrations of the falsehood of what is held by faith must be sophisms. It can, therefore, be taken for granted that any philosophic thesis which contradicts the teaching of revelation contains some sophism or other. Revealed truths are never indeed philosophic demonstrations of the falseness of some philosophic tenet, but they are the proof for the believer that the philosopher who upholds their falseness is deceived, and it belongs to philosophy alone to undeceive him.

There is here then an important point to learn. Theology, not primarily but secondarily and as it were accidentally, has, if occasion offers, to defend its own principles which are articles of faith.[1]   If a philosopher deny one article of faith, theology is very often able to convince him of the truth of what he denies by arguing with the aid of reason from some other article of faith admitted by the philosopher.   If, however, the philosopher admit no article of faith at all, then the help of reason is brought in to show the philosopher that on sheer dialectical grounds his argument contains some sophism, or that his argument is at best of only probable and not demonstrative certainty.

- Furthermore, the resources of philosophic speculation are also most useful to faith when it is a question of truths accessible to reason.   On the other hand, the body of philosophic doctrines to which in its entirety human reason would rarely attain if left to itself, is easily discovered for reason by the aid of faith, even though consequently reason may hold this body of truths on purely rational grounds.

We are now able to get a more precise notion of what is understood by the term theology.   Theology is a science. Like every other science it demonstrates its conclusions by the aid of reason; but it argues from premises that are ultimately known not like the first principles of reason by the light of reason, but by the light of revelation, and these principles are called articles of faith.

The material object with which both theology and the first philosophy is concerned, is God ; that is to say, God is the subject matter of both sciences.   But the formal object is in each case different.   The formal object of that branch of philosophy which treats of God are the conclusions demonstrated by reason and drawn from the first principles of reason ; but the formal object of theology are the conclusions demonstrated indeed by reason but drawn from principles that are revealed, called articles of faith.   The light or the means or the method (called the formal object *quo* in contradistinction to the preceding, which is called the formal object *quod*) by which such

[1] *Summa* I., Q. I., a. 8.

conclusions are drawn, likewise differs in both cases.   In
the case of philosophy the light or the formal object *quo*,
whereby conclusions are drawn, is the natural light of
reason ; in the case of theology this light or formal object
quo is revelation, which affects articles of faith directly
and the conclusions drawn indirectly.

It is evident then that reason is not only able to work
on revealed truths, but it must do so if we are to have a
theological science. Reason can bring forward all that
it itself has discovered by its natural power and apply its
reasoning to revealed truths, and thereby deduce conclusions which are the formal object *quod* of theology,
and are rightly called theological conclusions.

We have said that the light or the means whereby the
theologian draws his conclusions is revelation. ' Sacred
doctrine,' says St. Thomas,[1] ' considers no thing except
under this aspect, namely that it is *revealed by God.*'
Now the revelation of which St. Thomas speaks is not
immediate or direct revelation, but mediate, indirect, or
virtual. This is manifest, because the truths that are
immediately or directly revealed are not conclusions, they
are not scientific truths and cannot therefore be the object
of a *science* properly so-called.   It is of the very essence of a
science to acquire its truths by way of a rigorous deduction
from certain principles with the aid of reason.   Hence it
follows that a conclusion deduced from a principle which
is immediately revealed is not itself revealed in the same
degree, that is to say, immediately or directly.   The
conclusion, however, is revealed indirectly or virtually by
reason of the revealed principle which it involves, and is
consequently only mediately revealed, that is, through the
medium of reason which shows that it is included in the
principle.   The veritable object then of theological science
is the virtually revealed, or what are called theological
conclusions.[2]

Such being the intimate relation between philosophy

---

[1] *Summa* I., Q. I., a. 3.
[2] For an excellent discussion of the theological conclusion, cf. *Raymond-Martin O.P.   Revue Thomiste*, Janv.-Fevr. 1912.

and theology, it nevertheless remains that each has its own province of activity that is entirely distinct.

Firstly if, at times, their province of activity is common to both, they never coincide.

Theology is the science of truths necessary for our salvation ; now all truths are not necessary for salvation, and this is the precise reason why God does not reveal those truths concerning creatures (which truths we can learn of ourselves), if a knowledge of them is not necessary for our salvation.

There is then room outside Theology for a science which considers things in themselves, whereas theology considers them all as having reference, and only as having reference, to God and our salvation.

Further, even where the province of both faith and reason is the same, each retains its own specific character which assures its independence, for the procedure of each is entirely different which ever prevents their being confused together.

The philosopher derives his arguments from the essence of things and consequently from the proper causes of things ; on the contrary the theologian argues by mounting always to the first cause of things which is God, and he makes appeal to three different orders of argumentation which in every case would be considered as unsatisfactory by the philosopher as philosopher.

At times the theologian affirms a truth in the name of authority because it has been revealed by God ; at times, he affirms that the glory of God demands that such and such a thing is so, that is in the name of the principle of perfection ; again, at times he argues that such and such a thing is so because of the almighty power of God.[1]

A second difference to be noted, is manifest from the order faith and reason follow in the establishing of their conclusions. Philosophy considers creatures in themselves, and from them seeks to rise to the knowledge of God : hence the consideration of the creature comes first and that of God last. Theology, however, considers creatures only in so far as they have reference to God ; the contemplation

[1] *Cont. Gent.* Lib. II., Cap. 4.

of God comes first and that of the creature last. Wherefore theology follows an order which in itself is more perfect because it imitates the knowledge of God Himself; Who by knowing Himself knows all things.[1]

The attitude of St. Thomas with regard to faith and reason may then be summed up thus. With full knowledge of all the consequences entailed, St. Thomas accepts simultaneously both faith and reason. There is no effort on his part to effect as economically as possible a superficial conciliation between faith and those philosophic doctrines that are the more readily harmonized with the traditional teaching of theology. It is St. Thomas' thought that reason should develop its own province in full liberty, and according to the rigour that its method demands ; the philosophy that he teaches does not derive its scientific value from the fact that it is Christian, but from the fact that it is true in itself. The whole secret of Thomism lies in the immense effort of intellectual sincerity in reconstructing philosophy in such wise that its full accord *de facto* with theology appears as a necessary consequence of the rigorous demands of reason itself, rather than as the accidental result of a wished-for harmony.

Such seem to be the difference, the points of contact and the respective merits of faith and reason established by St. Thomas. Faith and reason cannot contradict each other, neither can they ignore each other, nor can they be confounded together. Reason may justify faith, but it can never transform it into reason ; faith may guide reason, but it can never transform reason into faith. It is then the very otherness of their essences which effects that one can act upon the other without detriment. A mixed state composed of reason and faith St. Thomas considers as contradictory and monstrous—it is like an animal composed of two different species.

Thomism then implies, in contradistinction to Augustinism for instance, that by the side of a philosophy that is nothing but philosophy, there is also a theology that is nothing but theology.

[1] *Cont. Gent.* Lib. II., Cap, 4.

F

II

The Fundamental Principle of the Thomistic System

ONE might say that the whole aim of theology, at least of human theology, is the salvation or the eternal happiness of the human soul. If this be so, it is evident that man must know God, know himself, and know the means of uniting himself to God. It is for this reason that St. Thomas divides his *Summa Theologica* into three parts, which treat respectively of God, of man, and of the God-man.

In the first part of the *Summa* St. Thomas treats of God's existence, nature, attributes and of the Holy Trinity, or of God's inner life. He proves that God is the first cause or the creator of all things, as the one from Whom all things come ; he treats of God also as the final cause of all or as the one to Whom all things must return.

In the second part of the *Summa* he treats of man, since among God's fallen creatures man alone is capable of redemption. Herein, therefore, he speaks of human behaviour, of the virtues and vices, and of law and of grace, both of which help man towards good behaviour.

The third part of the *Summa* treats of the God-man or Jesus Christ, through Whose infinite merits man is redeemed, and a way opened up for man's journey back to God.

Thus we have in a few words the plan of St. Thomas' theology epitomised in his immortal work the *Summa Theologica*.

The wonder of the theology of St. Thomas is its remarkable unity and solidarity of doctrine. We have already stated that the theology of St. Thomas is not divorced from his philosophy. Thomistic philosophy is the hand-maid of Thomistic theology. Whatever reason has discovered by argument from its own principles is brought forward by St. Thomas and made use of in his theology. In theology there is introduced a new element derived directly from revelation, but it is by means of reason with all its philosophic equipment that a theologic science is evolved. It follows therefore that St. Thomas' system of the whole of knowledge must be a most remarkable synthesis if there results the most perfect harmony and solidarity of thought between his philosophic and theologic speculations. In proportion as a system lacks unity, so much is it less of a system. Many theologians and philosophers have endeavoured to give systems of knowledge to the world, but on examination it is found that they lack the first essential of a system, *viz.* solidarity of thought in every department. It is evident therefore that the system of St. Thomas, which is conspicuous for its harmony and unity of doctrine, must be eminently constructive or synthetic. Every stone in the edifice must be in its proper place, and if the structure is to stand firm there must be some unifying principle or foundation upon which it is built.

The most cursory examination of Thomistic philosophy and theology shows that the essential doctrines of any one department are applications to various matter of a principle inculcated by Aristotle in his metaphysics. It is the principle of the real distinction between *act* and *potentiality*.

The first unfolding of this principle necessarily implies that that which is in a state of potentiality cannot cease to be in that state unless it be ' moved ' from that state by something which is in the state of act ; *e.g.* cold water has the potentiality to become hot, but it is impossible for cold water to become hot unless it be ' moved ' by something that actually possesses heat. It will readily be seen that this conclusion is immediately inferred from the real distinction between potentiality and act. Hence the principle in a more explicit way may be formulated thus : *Potentiality, which is really distinct from act, can never become act unless it be reduced to act by something which is in act.*

Now we maintain that the real distinction between potentiality and act is the fundamental principle of the entire Thomist system ; formulated and elucidated at the outset in metaphysics, it is applied without exception to the fundamental doctrines in every department of Thomist philosophy and theology.

A brief survey of the various departments of the Thomist system will show the rigorous application of this principle.

In Metaphysics.—The Thomist doctrine of the real distinction between essence and existence in created things, wherein essence is a potentiality and existence is an act, is an application of the principle ; likewise the real distinction between substance and accidents—substance is in potentiality to the accidents which are its acts or perfections ; likewise the doctrine concerning the nature of dimensive quantity, the essence of which is not that it actually extends the parts of a corporeal substance in place, *i.e.* in triple dimension, but that it distributes the parts of that substance within the substance itself (which internal parts are only potentially distributed in triple dimension by dimensive quantity), and that it has the capability or potentiality of *actually* extending those parts in place according to triple dimension. Upon this doctrine of the nature of dimensive quantity is founded the doctrine of the real presence of the whole body of Christ in a small consecrated host, also the doctrine of the birth of Christ from a virgin mother, of His passing into a room the doors being shut, etc. Likewise the doctrine of cause and effect, or the principle of causality; since an analysis of ' *that which begins to be* (effect) *must have a reason* (cause) *for its inception* ' shows the underlying great principle.

In Psychology.—The doctrine of the unity of the human composite, *viz.* that the intellectual soul is the substantial form of the body, and that it is the only form, is an application of the same principle. 'Prime matter,' a pure potentiality, which is informed by the intellectual soul (or act) receives from this act all that makes it body, and human body, and living. Through the same principle it follows that the faculties of intellect and will are really distinct from the substance of the soul, because they are the acts or perfections of the soul, which in regard to them is a potentiality. As a consequence it also follows not only that every faculty is really distinct from its object as potentiality to act, but also that, in regard to it *as object*, every faculty is passive, not active. Hence the important doctrine that the human intellect is a passive, not active, power in that it receives, and does not make its object of thought *as object*.

Further, the human will, which is the faculty of choice, must ultimately be moved to the very act of choosing by something which is in act ; and the reason is that before the act of choosing, the will is in a state of potentiality and must therefore be moved by something to the state of perfection which is choosing. Only God, the *Actus Purus*, moves the will to the very act of choosing ; if aught else did this the will, *ipso facto*, would cease to be free. This is the Thomistic doctrine of 'physical[1] premotion,' which is a rigorous application of the aforesaid fundamental principle.

In Cosmology.—In this department of applied metaphysics the fundamental question concerns the precise nature of body, as body. Applying the aforesaid principle, Thomism concludes that body, as body, is a composite of two principles, one of which is substantial form and the other 'prime matter.' 'Prime matter' is a pure potentiality, of which the substantial form is the act ; and between the two, as a consequence, there is a real distinction.

In Theodicy.—The classic proof for the existence of God, *viz.* the argument drawn from the existence of motion in the world, is nothing more than a rigorous application of the same principle. Motion is here taken in its widest

---

[1] Physical, *i.e.* real and efficient, precisely as opposed to moral.

sense, embracing not only local motion but every kind of
' passage from potentiality to act.'

In Ethics.—All the doctrines concerning habits and
their formation ; of the passions, of virtues and vices,
of laws, etc., have their mainstay in the same fundamental
principle.

In Theology.—It is sufficient to run through the *Summa*
to see that the same principle is fundamental in the doctrines concerning revelation and inspiration. By an
understanding of the same great principle it is argued that
God alone is pure act with no admixture of potentiality
whatsoever, whilst everything created contains both
potentiality and act. Further, it is concluded not only
that God's essence is identically the same as His existence,
but that His intellect and His will, His attributes of unity,
goodness, truth, His knowledge and love are likewise
identically the same as His essence.

The same principle underlies the whole doctrine concerning the mystery of the trinity of persons in God.

A further application is to be found in the treatise on
the angels, whose existence is really distinct from their
essence, whose minds and wills are really distinct from
their substance, etc. Further, according to St. Thomas the
sacraments are instrumental causes of grace ; they are
not mere channels through which grace is infused into the
soul ; they are real, efficient instrumental causes which
produce grace in the soul. In regard to the sacramental
grace that informs it, the soul is a potentiality (*potentia
obedientialis*) and grace is the act.

Further, St. Thomas' doctrine on actual grace is a
rigorous application of the same great principle. Just as
in the natural order the human will is ' physically '[1]
premoved by God to the act of choice, so in the supernatural order, an actual grace is nothing more than a
' physical ' premotion in that order. Thus Thomism, by a
relentless logic, applies the great principle to the doctrine
of actual grace.

[1] That is by a real, efficient, precisely as opposed to moral, influx.

For St. Thomas the theory of Molina or Suarez subverts the doctrines concerning God as the Prime Mover of all things, of causality, and of the great metaphysical principle (which is the first unfolding of the real distinction between act and potency) : *Potentiality which is really distinct from act can never become act unless it be reduced to act by something which is in act.* In 'short, for the sake of a difficulty in applied metaphysics (*i.e.* the freedom of the will under God's physical premotion) Molinism gainsays a principle already formulated and fixed in metaphysics, just as he who, on account of some difficulty in mixed mathematics, gainsays a principle of pure mathematics.

Any conclusion other than the one drawn above wrecks a system of the *whole* of knowledge in the mind of St. Thomas. It is owing to the consistent application of the grand fundamental principle aforesaid to every department of knowledge that St. Thomas bequeathed to the world a sublime system remarkable for its perfect unity, harmony, and solidarity of thought.

III

Application of the Fundamental Principle to the Infinite and the Finite

SINCE the third part of this paper has to do with the dogmatic theology of St. Thomas, we will confine our thoughts to St. Thomas' doctrine concerning the nature of God and His perfections, thereby showing the characteristic difference between the infinite and the finite.[1]

The principle upon which St. Thomas firmly builds his doctrine is nought else than an application of the fundamental principle of which we have treated in the second part of this paper.

The principle is stated thus : *In God essence is identical with existence ; in things, other than God, there is a real (extramental) distinction between their essence and existence.*

As already said, this principle is an application of the more fundamental principle of the real distinction between potency and act. But there are certain philosophers and theologians who are unwilling to admit the real distinction between essence and existence in things other than God, and who nevertheless admit the real distinction between potency and act.

We shall therefore show that unless this principle be true, it is impossible according to St. Thomas to establish the

---

[1] It may be objected that in this Part III. we have not treated of dogmatic theology precisely as theology, that is as a science deducing its conclusions from revealed premisses which are articles of faith. It would, perhaps, have been more advantageous to have taken the Trinity or the Incarnation and to have shown how, from these articles of faith, St. Thomas drew theological conclusions and formed wonderful treatises on the Trinity and the Incarnation. We have, however, taken matter from the first part of the *Summa* which treats ' *De Deo Uno* ' ; and it is quite by accident that the main truths of this treatise (God's existence, His infinity, the Creation, etc.) which are revealed should also be demonstrable by reason. On this account one should not be surprised to find our disquisition rather metaphysical than properly speaking theological.

characteristic note of difference between the finite and the infinite, and further that it is impossible to bring forward any demonstrative proof of creation.

In the *Summa Contra Gentes*, Lib. I., Cap. 22, St. Thomas expresses the first part of the principle in question thus : ' In God existence and essence are identical ' (*In Deo idem est esse et essentia*). In Lib. II., cap. 52 he formulates the second part of the principle thus : ' In every other being existence and that which exists differ ' (*In omnibus autem aliis . . . differt esse et quod est*).

St. Thomas gives six proofs to demonstrate the first part, and seven to demonstrate the second part.

In St. Thomas' own words this SUBLIME TRUTH is the root and *raison d'être* of all the perfections proper to the Creator, and of all those attributes which by analogy and by way of opposition we affirm of created things.[1]

If one would see how important and fundamental is this thesis in the doctrine of St. Thomas, one has but to open the *Summa Theologica* and read article III. of the Second Question (*Utrum Deus sit*) and compare the doctrine expounded therein with the first article of Question XLIV. (*Utrum sit necessarium omne ens esse creatum a Deo*). The thoughtful reader will discover that St. Thomas ascends by the five royal avenues [2] from the world of corporeal and sensible things and arrives at the First Immovable Mover,—the First Efficient Cause independent of all—the Necessary Being having within Itself the reason of Its existence—the First Being containing within Itself the fullness of perfection—the First Intelligence by which the whole universe is ordered.

By the same royal road St. Thomas descends from these heights, bringing with him the truth of creation demonstrated philosophically by the most rigorous logic. By his ascending journey St. Thomas demonstrates the existence of God : the necessary existence of a Being which has

---

[1] Cf. *Cont. Gent.*, Lib. I., Cap. 22.
[2] The five proofs for the existence of God, I. Pars, Q. II., a. 3.

neither efficient, nor exemplary, nor final cause : *Ens cui nihil est causa essendi.*

On returning from his journey St. Thomas proves that all existing things with all their attendant perfections proceed from God by creation as from their efficient cause and as from their supreme exemplary and ultimate final cause : *Ens cui nihil est causa essendi, est causa essendi omnibus quæ sunt et quæ quocumque modo sunt.*

Now what is the demonstrative proof of this conclusion, which attains to the uttermost reach of all philosophic speculation ?

St. Thomas' proof is as short and simple as it is profound and synthetic. It is this : ' It is necessary to say that the angels and all things whatsoever that are not God were created by God. For God alone is His existence ; but in other things the essence of a thing is distinct from its existence as was shown above (Q. 3, a. 4). Whence it is manifest that God alone is essential being *(ens per essentiam)*, whereas all other things are participated beings *(entia per participationem)*. But that which is by participation is caused by that which is by essence, as every burning thing is caused by fire. It is therefore necessary that the angels were created by God.' [1]

Such is the only argument by which St. Thomas proves the truth of creation in the *Summa Theologica.* Every other argument, whatsoever its form or procedure, is ultimately reducible to this fundamental proof. Even the three reasons obscurely formulated by Plato, Aristotle and Avicenna and brought out into their full light by St. Thomas in *De Potentia* (Q. 3, a. 5) are reducible to the same fundamental proof. Further, the six admirable proofs given by St. Thomas in the *Summa Contra Gentes* are likewise reducible to the same fundamental proof.

Now our object is to discover the basic principle upon which this fundamental proof for creation is founded. Let us proceed in this wise :—

Whether one admit or deny the real distinction between

[1] *Summa* I., Q. 61, 1.

existence and essence in things other than God, we assert that everybody must admit the following proposition : ' Whatever exists by participation is caused by that which exists by essence ' (*omne quod est per participationem causatur ab eo quod est per essentiam*).

If this proposition is not true, God would not be the only essential being (*ens per essentiam*), and all other things would not be beings by participation (*entia per participationem*). God therefore would not be the primal source of all beings, and there would be things which were not created by God.

Further, if the above proposition is not true, beings other than God would not be beings by participation (*entia per participationem*), for to be such, two conditions are necessary : 1st *to be caused*, for without this participated being is unintelligible ; 2nd, *to be caused by that which is being by essence*, otherwise there would be no participation of being.

In one word, there would be no beings by participation unless they were caused by that which exists essentially ; on the other hand, there would be no being essentially existent unless it be the cause of beings that exist by participation.

This doctrine may be more tersely expressed by the following fundamental proposition :—

God alone exists essentially or by essence ; all things else exist by participation.[1]

This proposition formulated in general terms must be admitted by all thinkers worthy of the name, whether they admit or no the real distinction between existence and essence in things other than God. The difficulty begins when one seeks to discover the fundamental and supreme reason why God is Being by essence and other things beings by participation. *Hoc opus, hic labor est.*

What then is the meaning of the expression *ens per essentiam*, essential being ? It means necessary, eternal,

---

[1] *Solus Deus est ens per essentiam, omnia autem alia sunt entia per participationem.*

immutable being, infinite in its perfections. On the other hand *ens par participationem*, participated being, means contingent and temporal being, limited in its perfections.

Now if one ask what is the root and ultimate reason of this necessity of existence and of these perfections without limit in *Being by Essence*,—and the root of the contingency and mutability and limited perfections in *Being by participation*, we reply that there can be no other root or ultimate reason than this, *In God essence and existence are identical : in things other than God, essence and existence really differ.*

In all things other than God there are to be found two real elements, the first of which (*essence*) in relation to the second (*existence*) is a *real potentiality*, and of which the second (*existence*) in relation to the first (*essence*) is a *real act.* From this real composition *in linea entis* results, formally constituted, being by participation. On the other hand, from the absolute identity of essence and existence one necessarily concludes Pure Act *in linea entis*,—and herein one discovers the true notion of *Being by essence* (*ens per essentiam*).

By his sublime metaphysical sense and marvellous penetration of thought, St. Thomas discovers in the concepts of act and potentiality *in linea entis* the ultimate *why*, the radical cause and reason of the contingency and mutability and limitation of participated being ; and in the absolute identity of essence and existence the ultimate *why* and supreme reason of Essential Being, essentially infinite in perfection.

Solus Deus est suum esse ; in omnibus autem aliis differt essentia rei et esse ejus (I. Pars. Q. 3, a. 4).

Now unless this doctrine of St. Thomas be held, it is impossible to find any characteristic note whereby the finite is distinguished from the infinite. The adversaries [1] of this doctrine assert that the radical difference between the finite and the infinite is to be found in the *contingence* of finite being and in its absolute dependence upon infinite being. If one ask for the reason of this contingency and

[1] Duns Scot, Suarez, Vasquez, etc.

of this *absolute dependence*, they reply that Infinite Being is the Creator of all finite being, and that all finite beings were made from nothing by the creative power of Infinite Being. They say that in God the identity of essence and existence is without all dependence (*absque dependentia ab alio*) ; in things other than God, this identity implies dependence with regard to God. For these theologians, therefore, the ultimate reason, the characteristic difference between things and God is that all things depend upon Him : *Dependentia rerum omnium a Deo.*

Hence it is manifest that the adversaries of St. Thomas are arguing in a vicious circle ! They prove the necessity of creation from the contingency of finite things, and the contingency of finite things from the fact of their creation!

Everything depends on God because everything is created, and everything is created by God because everything depends upon God !

Everything except God is contingent and finite, because everything in order to exist demands necessarily the creative action of God,—and everything in order to exist requires the creative action of God because everything excepting God is finite and contingent !

Further, unless one admit the real distinction between essence and existence in things one cannot prove that all beings, God excepted, are finite unless one supposes they are created,—in the same way one cannot prove that God is infinite unless one suppose He is creator.

It is true that by this means it can be demonstrated that God is *infinite in His Being.* Given the fact of creation, this fact is sufficient to establish demonstratively that God's power is infinite. Creation necessarily demands an infinite power in the creative cause since the effect produced although finite in its reality, nevertheless demands an infinite power owing to its mode of production, which is a passage from nothing to being.[1]

But the difficulty always remains. How can one prove that God is the creator of all things ? How comes it that

[1] *Summa*, I. Pars, Q. 45, a. 5, ad 3.

things in order to exist, must be created by God and receive from Him the act of existence ?

For St. Thomas there is no other means of answering these questions unless one admit the fundamental truth : *In God existence is identical with essence ; in all things else existence is really distinct from essence.*[1]

This identity of existence and essence in God according to St. Thomas is proper to God alone ; it is proper to Him in the same way as the attributes of necessary being, of first mover, of supreme being—of Pure Act *in linea entis.* It is from this identity of existence and essence that St. Thomas sets out to infer the other Divine attributes and in particular the attribute of Infinite Being and Its unity. Following upon this he demonstrates that all beings were produced by God, the Essential Being, as regards all the participated reality they possess. That is to say, that all things were produced by God from nothing, wholly, without presupposition whatsoever of anything from which they were formed.

Thus taking his point of departure from the identity in God of existence and essence, and inferring therefrom the notion of infinite being and of the unity of infinite being, St. Thomas is enabled to demonstrate the truth of creation. *Necesse est omne ens quod quocumque modo est, a Deo esse creatum.*

Hence the ultimate ' Why ', the supreme sufficient reason of the absolute infinity of the Divine perfections is the real identity of essence and existence in God. The ultimate sufficient reason of the finite character of created things with their limited perfections is that they are composed, really, of essence and existence. St. Thomas establishes this doctrine by the most rigorous reasoning.[2] Thus do the great commentators of St. Thomas interpret his thought. Cajetan, Sylvester Ferrariensis, and John of St. Thomas (to mention only three) from an analysis

---

[1] *In Deo non est aluid essentia ejus ; in omnibus autem aliis differt essentia rei et esse ejus.* Summa, I Pars, Q. 3, a. 6, ad 1 ; and Q. 7, a. 2, ad 1.

[2] *Cont. Gent.* Lib. II., Cap. 52.

of the idea of infinite being agree in affirming that the characteristic note of infinite being consists in the real identity of essence and existence.[1]

It is therefore impossible, according to St. Thomas, to demonstrate that a thing is created unless in that thing there is a composition of act and potency *in linea entis.* Herein we discover the characteristic note of finite being. To try to explain the Divine attributes without having recourse to the absolute identity between essence and existence in God, or to explain the attributes of creatures without having recourse to the real distinction between their essence and existence, is to remove the only foundation upon which the philosophic demonstration of creation is based.

St. Thomas has synthesised this most profound doctrine in a simple sentence : *Subsistent Being is the cause of all received being.*[2]

Existence is the act of every perfection. If there are no limits either on the part of the subject or on the part of the predicate, all perfections will be contained in a pre-eminent way in Pure Act which contains all acts and all forms, and in which all perfections are only one perfection of absolute simplicity. In *Subsistent Being* there can be no limits on the part of the subject, since the substance of the subject which exists is identical with its existence. Hence in the proposition : *God exists*, the reality signified by the word *God* is the same as the reality signified by the word *Exists.*

Further, there can be no limits on the part of the predicate, since all perfections are *included* in Subsistent Being ; hence there can be no accidental perfection in God. *To be* and *to be wise*, *to be* and *to be good* are identical in God just as the Divine substance is identical with existence :

---

[1] For *Cajetan*, cf. Comm. in I. Part, Q. 7, a. 1 ; and Q. XII., a. 11. For *Sylv. Ferrariensis*, cf. Comm. in *Cont. Gent.*, Lib. I., Cap. 42, and Lib. II., Cap. 52. For *Joan. a S. Thomâ*, cf. Cursus Theol. T. I., Q. VIII., primæ Part, disp. 7, a. 1.

[2] *Esse per se subsistens est causa omnis esse in alio recepti*, Q. VII., a. 1, ad 1.

and the same is to be said with regard to all the Divine attributes.

On the contrary, *received existence* or *participated existence* is limited, circumscribed, made to the measure, and corresponding to the capacity of the nature of which it is the act. *By the very fact* that this existence is really distinct from the essence or the substance, every subsequent act or perfection is limited, finite, and accidental. The real distinction between existence and essence implies consequently the distinction, also real, of all other acts or accidental perfections.

Distinct from each other these acts or perfections are also distinct from the subject or substance which sustains and unites them. Hence, in man for instance, *to be* and *to be wise, to be* and *to be good,* etc., are really distinct.

It follows then that the Divine Existence is the very substance of God. But the existence of the creature is distinct from its substance ; it is an act received into the substance and completing this substance *in linea entis.*

From this composition of *act* and *potency in linea entis,* results finite being, limited by a specific nature of which existence is the act. From the union of these two real elements results created being. The essence of a created being is a capacity for existence (*potentia essendi*) ; the substance of God is existence (Esse).

For this reason the words *Subsistent Being* (*Esse Subsistens, Ipsum esse, qui Est, Javeh*) express the grandeur of God, the fullness and the immensity of His Being, the infinite character of His attributes, the sublimity of His perfections, and the sovereignty and ineffableness of His unity.

Nulla de perfectionibus essendi potest deesse Ei quod est ipsum esse subsistens.[1] Hoc autem simplex unum et sublime est ipse Deus.[2]

[1] *Summa*, I. Pars., Q. IV., a. 2.
[2] S. Thomas *In lib. Boetii de Hebdom.*, c. II.

The Mysticism of St. Thomas Aquinas

By Fr. Vincent McNabb, O.P.

HIS Holiness Pope Pius XI., in his Encyclical Letter, *Studiorum Ducem*, has given us words of official weight which will serve as introduction to our own halting words of commentary. After having spoken of St. Thomas as the master in both Philosophy and in Apologetic, Dogmatic and Moral Theology, His Holiness adds : ' Nor is his *ascetical* and *mystical* science any less noble. He reduces the whole of moral discipline to the virtues and gifts ; and he excellently defines the same method and discipline for various states of life, whether for those who follow the ordinary Christian life or for those who strive after consummate perfection, whether in a contemplative or active order.

' Therefore if we wish to understand the first commandment and its extent, and how charity and the accompanying gifts increase ; if we would know all the many states of life, for instance, of perfection, the religious, the apostolate, and in what they differ and what is their nature and force ; if we are seeking to know these and such points of ascetic and mystical theology, we must first of all approach the Angelic Doctor.' (*Litt. Ency.* ' *Studiorum Ducem*,' 29 June, 1923.)

His Holiness has here suggested that Practical Theology has three divisions, which are in series. These three parts of Practical Theology are Moral, Ascetical and Mystical. It would be hazardous to say what is meant by Mystical Theology ; seeing that accredited writers, while agreeing that Mystical Theology is not Moral nor Ascetical, disagree as to what it is. We shall therefore leave untouched what is meant, and merely set down what we mean, by Mystical Theology. In the words of Ribet : ' The Science of

G

Mysticism is a science which groups and formulates as a body of doctrine the facts and the laws regarding supernatural communications.'[1] We shall therefore endeavour to show (A) that St. Thomas gives the ultimate laws of Mystical Theology ; and (B) that St. Thomas gives the proximate laws of Mystical Theology.

A. St. Thomas Gives the Ultimate Laws of Mystical Theology.

As the Science of Mystical Theology is not primary but derivative, it borrows its laws or principles from the primary sciences. For this reason the scientific mystic, to claim our serious attention, must be acquainted with the fundamental principles of the sciences which Mystical Theology presupposes. Errors in these preliminary sciences, though often of no consequence to the empiric mystic, are rarely of no consequence to the mystical thinker or writer. The annals of false Mysticism within the body of Roman Catholics themselves, are strewn with records of men whose errors in Philosophy or Theology ended by becoming errors in their mystical teaching. But, indeed, we need not press a point which is at least implicitly accepted by those ethical teachers who agree that nothing is of more importance than the basis of their ethics.

Now it goes without saying that St. Thomas is without a rival, almost without a second, in the completely welded synthesis of his philosophical and theological thought. At the base of his Mystical Theology rests a sound and profound Psychology. This equips him in a unique way for the task of writing scientifically on Mysticism ; since without a knowledge of psychology a writer may give us some mystical facts, but not the Science of Mystical Theology. St. Thomas had deeply meditated on the need of a true psychology as a basis of the other sciences. In the introduction to his commentary on Aristotle's 'ΠΕΡΙ

[1] M. J. Ribet : *La Mystique Divine*. Paris, 1895. P. 21.

ΨΥΧΗΣ' he wrote : ' The knowledge of the soul would seem to be of great service to all the truths taught by the other sciences. It has something to give all parts of philosophy. . . . As regards Moral Philosophy, we cannot rightly reach the science of Morals unless we know the powers of the soul. . . . Hence in his Ethics the philosopher assigns the several virtues to the several powers of the soul.' (*De Anima*, lib. I., lect. I.)

It is therefore significant that St. John of the Cross, one of the most accredited writers on Mystical Theology, was influenced by the psychology of St. Thomas. According to his English biographer, St. John of the Cross ' does not seem to have ever applied himself to the study of the Fathers.' [1] ' It has been recorded that during his studies he particularly relished psychology, this is amply borne out by his writings. St. John was not what one would term a scholar. He was, however, intimately acquainted with the *Summa* of St. Thomas Aquinas, as almost every page of his works proves ' (p. 13). Again : ' The key to the whole treatise ' [*Ascent of Mount Carmel*] ' will be found in the seventh chapter of the second book of the *Ascent*. As has already been stated, the whole work is based upon the view St. Thomas takes of the essence and operations of the senses, and upon his treatise on the virtues ' (p. 17).

In other words, the great Spanish Mystical writer bases his Mystical Science on the *Summa* of St. Thomas, and especially on that psychological teaching which makes the *Summa* the classic guide to Psychology.

But if Psychology is needed, still more is *Dogmatic* Theology needed for scientific Mysticism. Not everyone who discusses with his contemporaries the problems and phenomena of Mysticism, has realised how wise the experts have been in applying the dogmatic test to Mystical phenomena. These experts, who were often taken to be inconsequent in their dogmatic test, were merely asserting

---

[1] *The Ascent of Mt. Carmel*, by St. John of the Cross. Prefatory Essay by Benedict Zimmerman, O.C.D. London, Thomas Baker, 1906. P. 10.

the principle that if there is ' a father of lies,' and therefore a pseudo-mysticism, the true Mysticism cannot rest on a dogmatic untruth. The history of all forms of pseudo-mysticism is but a statistical corroboration of the principle that any error in the dogmatic basis of human action will lead inevitably to great harm in matters of the soul. For this reason it cannot be too often asserted that the most important section of the Ten Commandments is not any of the Commandments, but the dogmatic basis of all the Commandments : ' I AM THE LORD THY GOD.'

But if to be a skilled scientific Mystical teacher demands a scientific knowledge of dogmatic truths, none of the Church's teachers has so much authority as the genius and saint, Thomas Aquinas, whose synthesis of theology is unique and unchallenged.

Moreover, St. Thomas has in a supreme degree the last necessary qualification for a teacher of scientific Mysticism. He is the master of Ethics or Moral Theology. Indeed, as we have pointed out elsewhere,[1] he may be said to have created Moral Theology. What he added to Greek thought in the sphere of Metaphysics and Psychology is as nothing to what he added in the sphere of Ethics. This would give him rank as a safe teacher of Mystical Theology. Wrong theories of Ethics are hardly less fundamental and rarely less harmful than wrong views of Dogmatics. To realise what wild inhuman views can be called Mysticism, we need only read the list of mystical principles of Molinos. Rarely has human depravity reached such explicit formulation as in the doctrines of this Roman spiritual director who was ignorant of the principles of Ethics.

Therefore as St. Thomas Aquinas has no rival in the sphere of Psychology, Dogmatic and Moral Theology, he is the most sure guide in the matter of Mystical Theology by formulating, as no other writer has succeeded in formulating, the ultimate laws of Mystical Theology.

---

[1] Xenia Thomistica.

B. St. Thomas Formulates the Proximate Laws of Mystical Theology.

We are here overladen with the wealth of St. Thomas' mystical teaching. In our despair of giving our readers a true idea of what St. Thomas has bequeathed to them, we must content ourselves with something little better than a mere list or catalogue of our inheritance.

From Psychology St. Thomas has taken the accurate division of the sensitive and intellectual, the cognoscitive and appetitive powers of the soul. Whilst he is always scientific in maintaining that all our [natural] knowledge comes to us through the senses, and that our intellectual knowledge is an elaboration of sensible knowledge by the active intellect ; yet he has a firm grasp of the passive— or what he calls the obediential—powers of the human intellect to receive knowledge without sensible imagery. Thus is speaking of the soul when separated from the body, he says: ' But when it is separated from the body it understands no longer by turning to phantasms but by turning to simple intelligible objects.' [1ᵃ, Qu. 89, Art. 2. Eng. tr.] This doctrine he applies to the infused or prophetic and therefore mystical knowledge of Jesus Christ. He says : ' Christ's intellect, in regard to His infused knowledge, could understand without turning to phantasms.' [3ᵃ, Qu. 34, Art. 2, ad 3. Eng. tr.] And in this matter of mystical, infused knowledge the intellect of the mystic would be as the human intellect of Jesus Christ.

The importance of this doctrine may be judged from the following words of St. John of the Cross : ' *In this serene night*, that is, Contemplation, in which the soul desires to behold the grove. It is called night because the Contemplation is obscure ; and that is the reason why it is called Mystical Theology, that is, the secret or hidden science of God, wherein God without the sound of words or the intervention of any bodily or spiritual sense, as it were in silence and in repose, in the darkness of sense and nature, teaches the soul—and the soul knows not why—

in a most secret and hidden way. Some spiritual writers call this *understanding without understanding*, because it does not take place in what philosophers call the Active Intellect, which is conversant with the forms, fancies and apprehensions of the physical faculties, but in the Intellect, as it is Passive, which without receiving such forms, receives passively only the substantial intelligence of them free from all imagery.' [St. John of the Cross, *ut sup.*— *A Spiritual Canticle*, p. 208.] It will here be seen that in defining the very essence of Mystical Theology the Spanish Mystic of the sixteenth century is doing little more than comment on the doctrine St. Thomas had already taught authoritatively three centuries before.

Another fundamental mystical principle of St. Thomas is the supremacy of Charity or the love of God. This is all the more striking because St. Thomas was clear in asserting the supremacy of the intellect over the will. But his ' doctrine ' is too profound to be given in any words but his own. In answer to the question ' Whether the Will is a higher power than the Intellect,' he says : ' The superiority of one thing over another can be considered . . . absolutely and relatively. . . . Therefore, since the proper nature of a power is in its order to an object, it follows that the intellect in itself and absolutely is higher and nobler than the will. . . .

' But . . . when the thing in which is good is nobler than the soul itself in which is the idea understood, by comparison with such a thing, the will is higher than the intellect. But when the thing which is good is less noble than the soul, then even in comparison with that thing the intellect is higher than the will.

' Wherefore the love of God is better than the knowledge of God ; but on the contrary, the knowledge of corporeal things is better than the love thereof. Absolutely, however, the intellect is nobler than the will.' [1ª, Qu. 82, Art. 3.]

This supremacy of charity or love is one of the many interpretative principles of the Mystical Theology of St.

Thomas. In his elaboration of it, no writer is his equal.
He has given us a perfect study of another aspect of this
principle in words of such simplicity that we may overlook
their depth. 'Something is required for the perfection
of knowledge that is not requisite for the perfection of
love. For knowledge belongs to reason, whose function
consists in distinguishing things which are in reality
united, and in reuniting together after a fashion things
that are distinct, by comparing them with another. Consequently the perfection of knowledge requires that man
should know distinctly all that is in a thing, such as its
parts, powers, and properties. On the other hand love
is in the appetitive power which regards a thing as it is in
itself; wherefore it suffices for the perfection of love that
a thing be loved according as it is known in itself. Hence
it is that a thing may be loved more than it is known;
since it can be loved perfectly even without being perfectly
known. This is most evident in regard to the sciences,
which some love through having a certain general knowledge of them : for instance, they know that rhetoric is a
science that enables man to persuade others; and this
is what they love in rhetoric. The same applies to the
love of God.' [1ᵃ, 2ᵃᵉ, Qu. 27, Art. 2, ad 2.]
    Yet this supremacy of love does not mean that we are as
certain of our love as of our faith. The affective union
with God if more noble is more mysterious and unnamed
than is the cognoscitive union. St. Thomas says : 'It
is an essential condition of knowledge that a man should
have certitude of the objects of knowledge, and, again,
it is an essential condition of faith that a man should be
certain of the things of faith, and this because certitude
belongs to the perfection of the intellect, wherein these
gifts exist. Hence whoever has knowledge or faith is
certain that he has them. But it is otherwise with grace
and charity and suchlike, which perfect the appetitive
faculty.' [1ᵃ, 2ᵃᵉ, Qu. 112, Art. 5, ad 2.]
    Now fundamental Mystical Theology may be seen from
the following words of St. Teresa in her *Relations* : 'When

all the powers are united they cannot do anything whatever ; the understanding is as it were stupified ; *the will
loves more than it understands ; but it does not understand
if it is loving ; nor what it is doing in such a way as to put
it into words.'* [*Relations,* 5th.] St. Teresa here instinctively follows the doctrine of St. Thomas. Even the
presence of charity in the soul is not directly perceived !

Another Mystical principle which can be easily and
disastrously misapplied is the principle of *Passivity.*
Historians of Mystical Theology will recall with a
shudder the obscene quietistic doctrine of Molinos, of
whom Dom. B. Mackey, the editor of works of St. Francis
of Sales, has written : ' Molinos s'était fixé a Rome en
1665, l'année même de la canonisation de saint François de
Sales et y publia en 1671 sa Guide Spirituelle, dans laquelle
il prétendait s'appuyer sur la doctrine de notre Saint '
[*i.e.* St. Francis of Sales] ' ce principe base de tout son
systeme :—l'âme parfaite doit supprimer tout acte de la
volonté et de l'entendement et anéantir ses puissances.'
[*Oeuvres de Saint François de Sales.* Annecy 1874. Introd.
by Dom. B. Mackey, O.S.B. Vol. IV., p. lvii.]

A propos of Molinos' plea that he borrowed his principle
from St. Francis of Sales, perhaps the most interesting
passage from the Saint is the following : ' Ce repos ' [*i.e.*,
de l'Ame recuillie en son Bienaymé] ' passe quelquefois
si avant en sa tranquillité que toute l'âme et toutes les
puissances d'icelle demeurent comme endormies, sans
faire aucun mouvement, ni action quelconque sinon la
seule volonté, laquelle même ne fait aucun autre chose
sinon recevoir l'ayse et la satisfaction que la presence du
Bienaymé lui donne . . .   la volonté n'appercoit point
cet ayse et contentement qu'elle recoit jouissant insen-
siblement d'iceluy ; d'autant qu'elle ne pense pas à soi
mais à celuy la presence duquel lui donne ce plaisir.'
[*Ibid. Traitté de l'Amour de Dieu,* Liv. VI., ch. vii.]

Light is thrown on this dark saying of St. Francis by the
following extract from St. Thomas' treatise on Prophecy ;
a treatise of supreme importance to all scientific study

of Mystical phenomena. In answer to the question whether prophecy is a habit in the prophets, St. Thomas says that ' properly speaking, prophecy is not a habit. . . . However prophecy may be reduced to a passion, provided we understand passion to denote any kind of receiving, in which sense the Philosopher says [*De Anima* iii.] that *to understand is, in a way, to be passive.* For just as in natural knowledge the possible intellect is passive to the light of the active intellect, so too in prophetic knowledge the human intellect is passive to the enlightening of the Divine light.' [2ª, 2ªᵉ, Qu. 171, 2, ad 1m.]

It would have been well for the Church had the controversialists on Quietism stated their doctrine in terms of receptivity rather than passivity. Unfortunately our modern minds have been so attuned to the terminology of physical science that to be passive means to have no action, nor indeed activity or act. Had men grasped the doctrine which St. Thomas borrowed from Artistole, namely that to be passive merely means to receive, men could easily have agreed that there is a mystical union with God so transcendant that the mystical *act* or activity (of intelligence and will) is received from the bounty of God.

Again, the key to this deep mystical doctrine is the doctrine of the seven Gifts of the Holy Ghost. It is hardly an exaggeration to say that the Science of these gifts in themselves and in their relationship to the mystical life is the creation of St. Thomas. With an insight for series and for scientific unity he has based these gifts on psychology and ethics. We have but to compare his treatment of them with the treatment they receive from any of his predecessors in order to understand our debt to his genius. His short treatise on the Gifts in general, which he has included in the larger treatise on Habits, must be studied and grasped by every serious student of Mystical Theology. What could be more simple or luminous than the following : ' In man there is a two-fold principle of movement— one within him, *viz.* the reason; the other extrinsic to him, *viz.* God. Now it is evident that whatever is moved must be proportionate to its mover ; and the perfection of the mobile, as such, consists in a disposition whereby it is disposed to be well moved by its mover. Hence the more exalted the mover, the more perfect must be the disposition whereby the mobile is made proportionate to its mover. Thus we see that a disciple needs a more perfect disposition in order to receive a higher teaching from his master.

' Now it is manifest that human virtues perfect man according as it is natural for him to be moved by his reason in his interior and exterior actions. Consequently man needs yet higher perfections, whereby to be disposed to be moved by God. These perfections are called gifts not only because they are infused by God, but also because by them man is disposed to become amenable to the Divine inspiration.' [1ᵃ, 2ᵃᵉ, Qu. 68, Art. 1.]

We despair of conveying to our readers the depth and precision of this foundation principle of Mystical Theology. Though the words are so simple in meaning and arrangement as to appear of axiomatic clearness, yet their full understanding demands much preliminary study. For instance, St. Thomas makes use of the words ' inspiration ' and ' moved by God.' These apparently simple words demand the preliminary and profound treatise on the operations of the mind and will by their own natural powers and under the movement of the Divine will.

It is particularly in his treatise on the Gift of Wisdom that St. Thomas has given a supreme scientific guidance to writers of Mystical Theology. Thus in answer to his own question *Whether Wisdom is merely speculative and practical also ?* he writes : ' The higher a virtue is the greater the number of things to which it extends, as stated by *De Cavsis*. Wherefore from the very fact that wisdom as a gift is more excellent than wisdom as an intellectual virtue, since it attains to God more intimately by a kind of union of the soul with Him, it is able to direct us not only in contemplation but in action. . . .

' Divine things are indeed necessary and eternal in themselves. Yet they are the rules of the contin-

gent things which are the subject-matter of human
actions. . . .

'A thing is considered in itself before its being compared
with something else. Wherefore to wisdom belongs first
of all contemplation, which is the vision of the beginning
and afterwards the direction of human act according to
the Divine rules. Nor from the direction of wisdom does
there result any bitterness or toil in human acts ; on the
contrary the result of wisdom is to make the bitter sweet
and labour a rest.' [2ª, 2ᵃᵉ, Qu. 45, Art. 3, ad 1, 2, 3.]

Perhaps the most searching test of the trustworthiness
of a mystical writer is his expression of the presence of
God in the soul. Here again St. Thomas has done little
less than formulate the principles of accurate expression.
Thus in treating of the question '*Whether man can know
that he has grace?*' he says : 'The things that are in the
soul by their physical reality are known through experi-
mental knowledge, in so far as through acts man has
experience of their inward principles ; thus when we wish
we perceive that we have a will, and when we exercise
the functions of life, we observe that there is life is us. . . .
No one can know he has the knowledge of a conclusion
if he does not know its principle. But the principle of
grace and its object is God, Who by His very excellence
is unknown to us. . . . And hence His presence in
us and His absence cannot be known with certainty'
. . . (except) 'by revelation.' [Iª, 2ᵃᵉ, Qu. 112,
Art. 5.]

The same intricate problem of knowing God's presence
in the soul would have led to fewer ontologistic explanations if writers had carefully weighed the doctrine of St.
Thomas on the direct vision of God in the First Part of the
Summa. For example, St. Thomas says, ' It is evident
how the glorified eyes will see God as now our eyes see the
life of another. But life is not seen with the corporeal
eye, as a thing in itself visible, but as the indirect object of
the sense ; which indeed is not known by sense but at
once, together with sense, by some other cognitive power.

But that the Divine presence is known by the intellect immediately on the sight of and through corporeal things, happens from two causes, *viz.* from the perspicuity of the intellect, and from the refulgence of the Divine glory infused into the body after its renovation.' [1ᵃ, Qu. 12, Art. 3, ad 2.]

In modern times there has been a praiseworthy attempt to distinguish clearly between genuine mystical phenomena and mental phenomena of an abnormal or pathological character. One of the chief tests of the genuine character of mystical phenomena is the rapid return of the mystic from its extraordinary to its normal state. St. Thomas has words of deep psychological insight in his question ' *Whether prophetic vision is always accompanied by abstraction from the senses ?* ' He says, ' the spirit of the prophets is said to be subject to the prophets as regards the prophetic utterances . . . because . . . the prophets in declaring what they have seen, speak their own mind, and are not thrown off their mental balance like persons who are possessed.' [2ᵃ, 2ᵃᵉ, Qu. 173, Art. 3, ad 4.]

Much of the teaching of St. John of the Cross is based, perhaps without his knowing that it is based, on the following principle : ' When a man knows that he is being moved by the Holy Ghost to think something or signify something by word or deed, this belongs properly to prophecy ; whereas when he is moved without his knowing it, this is not perfect prophecy but a prophetic instinct. Nevertheless it will be observed that since the prophet's mind is a defective instrument, even true prophets know not all that the Holy Ghost means by the things they see or speak or even do.' [*Ibid.*, Art. 4.]

Psychology has rarely been made to serve Mystical Theology so well as in the article ' *Whether the operation of Contemplation is fittingly divided into a threefold movement— Circular, Straight, and Oblique ?* ' The whole article is but an expert scientific commentary on a passage from ' *the Divine Name* ' of Dionysius. St. Thomas lays down the following distinctions, which can be overlooked only to the

great hurt of sound Mystical Theology : ' External bodily
movements are opposed to the quiet of contemplation,
which consists in rest from outward occupation ; but the
movements of intellectual operations belong to the quiet
of contemplation.' [2, 2^{ae}, Qu. 180, Art. 6, ad 1.]

Again : ' Man is like the angels in intellect generally,
but the intellective power is much higher in the angel
than in man. Consequently these movements must be
ascribed to men and angels, in different ways according
as they are differently related to uniformity.

CIRCULAR.—' For the *angelic* intellect has uniform
knowledge in two respects. First, because it does not
acquire intelligible truth from the variety of composite
objects ; secondly, because it understands the truth of
intelligible objects not discursively but by simple intuition.

' On the other hand the intellect of the *soul* acquires
intelligible truth from sensible objects, and understands
it by a certain discoursing of reason.

' Wherefore Dionysius assigns the CIRCULAR movement
of the angels to the fact that their intuition of God is
uniform and unceasing, having neither beginning nor end ;
even as circular movement, having neither beginning nor
end, is uniformly around the one same centre.

' But on the part of the soul, ere it arrive at this
uniformity, its twofold lack of uniformity needs to be
removed—first, that which arises from the variety of
external things ; this is removed by the soul withdrawing
from externals, and so the first thing he mentions regarding
the circular movement of the soul is *the soul's withdrawal
into itself from external objects*. Secondly, another lack of
uniformity requires to be removed from the soul ; and
this is owing to the discoursing of reason. This is done by
directing all the soul's operations to the simple contemplation of the intelligible truth ; and this is indicated by his
saying in the second place that the *soul's intellectual
powers must be uniformly concentrated*, in other words that
discoursing must be laid aside and the soul's gaze fixed
on the contemplation of the one simple truth. In this

operation of the soul there is no error, even as there is clearly no error in the understanding of first principles which we know by simple intuition.   Afterwards, these two things being done, he mentions thirdly the uniformity which is like that of the angels, for then all things being laid aside the soul continues in the contemplation of God alone. This he expresses by saying : *Then being thus made uniform unitedly, i.e. conformably, by the union of its powers it is conducted to the good and the beautiful.'*

STRAIGHT.—'The *straight* movement of the *Angels* cannot apply to his proceeding from one thing to another by considering them ; but only to the order of his providence, namely, to the fact that the higher angel enlightens the lower angels through the angels that are intermediate . . .

'Whereas he ascribes the straight movement in the *soul* to the soul's proceeding from exterior sensibles to the knowledge of intelligible objects.'

OBLIQUE.—'The oblique movement in the *Angels* he describes as being composed of the straight and circular movements, inasmuch as their care for those beneath them is in accordance with their contemplation of God.

'While the oblique movement in the *soul* he also declares to be partly straight and partly circular, in so far as in reasoning it makes use of the light received from God.' [2ᵃ, 2ᵃᵉ, Qu. 180, Art. 6, ad 2.]

The appeal made by this profound psychology of Dionysius may be measured by the Saint's answer to the third objection.   Against the division made by Dionysius into the threefold movement, *viz.* circular, straight and oblique.   St. Thomas objects to the division made by Richard of St. Victor in his famous work *' On Contemplation.'*

Few writers on Mystical Theology had as much weight with the thirteenth century and with the University of Paris as had this most distinguished son of the University. Yet when his authority is pitted against that of Dionysius, St. Thomas endeavours not to make the earlier writer agree with the later, but to bring the later into line with the earlier. And the Dumb Ox, who is so seldom stirred to warmth in his expression, closes the camparison between Dionysius and Richard of St. Victor by the curt phrase, ' Wherefore it is evident that Dionysius describes the movement of contemplation with much greater fulness and depth (*multo sufficientius et subtilius*).' [*Ibid.* ad 3.]

The profound scientific humility of St. Thomas is altogether in his teaching on the gift of wisdom. He writes : ' Wisdom denotes a certain rectitude of judgment according to the Eternal Law. Now rectitude of judgment is twofold : first, on account of perfect use of reason ; secondly, on account of a certain connaturality with the matter about which one has to judge. Thus about matters of chastity a man after inquiring with his reason forms a right judgment if he has learnt the Science of Morals, whilst he who has the habit of chastity judges of such matters by a kind of connaturality.

' Accordingly it belongs to the wisdom that is an intellectual virtue to pronounce right judgment about divine things after reason has made its enquiry. But it belongs to wisdom as a gift of the Holy Ghost to judge aright about them on account of connaturality with them. Thus Dionysius says (*Divine Names* ii.) that "*Hierotheus is perfect in divine things, for he not only learns but is patient of divine things.*"

' Now this sympathy or connaturality for divine things is the result of charity which unites us to God, according to I. *Cor.* vi. 17 : " *He who is joined to the Lord is one spirit.*" Consequently wisdom which is a gift has its cause in the will, which cause is charity. But it has its essence in the intellect, whose act is to judge aright.' [2ᵃ, 2ᵃᵉ, Qu. 45, Art. 2.] The doctrine here set forth, and largely originated by St. Thomas, is so rich in thought that subsequent writers on Mystical Theology have not yet exhausted its wealth. To us a main interest in the doctrine of this greatest of theologians is his chivalrous championship of the average Christian ; whose gift of the Holy Ghost is even a higher wisdom than the highest acquirement of the Schools.

That this championship is not a passing mood but an abiding conviction may be proved by its recurrence in the *Summa*. Thus he deals with it again in asking the question ' *Whether there can be moral without intellectual virtue ?* ' [1ᵃ, 2ᵃᵉ, Qu. 58, Art. 4.] His conclusion is that there can be no moral virtue without the intellectual virtues of prudence and understanding.

To this he objects the obvious fact that some men are ' virtuous and acceptable to God without being vigorous in the use of reason.' His answer is a valuable fragment of mediaeval wisdom. He says, ' A man may be virtuous without having the use of reason as to everything ; provided he have it in those things which have to be done virtuously. In this way all virtuous men have full use of reason. Hence those who seem simple through lack of worldly cunning may yet be prudent, according to Matt. x. 16 : ' *Be ye therefore prudent as serpents and simple as doves* ' [ad 2ᵐ].

These scholarly, humble words of St. Thomas Aquinas recall the famous epigram of another Thomas in the opening sentences of *The Imitation of Christ*, ' Opto magis sentire compunctionem quam scire ejus definitionem' [I would rather feel compunction than know its definition. —*De Imitat. Christi*, lib. I, ch. I.] Some lovers of the *Imitation* have seen in these witty words of the Belgian ascetic an indictment of the scholastic thinkers and theologians. But the indictment could be substantiated only by indicting the epigrammatist himself with ignorance of the profound scientific humility of the Prince of Scholastics.

A further championship of the average Christian, and indeed of the simpler folk, is to be found in an article which might well be put as an introduction to every book of or on Meditation. St. Thomas asks the question *Whether Contemplation or Meditation is the cause of Devotion*. No summary of an article which is itself a perfect summary would do anything but mutilate a masterpiece. To his question he gives the answer that meditation, and therefore still more contemplation, is a cause of devotion. Against this doctrine he urges the objection : ' If contemplation were the proper cause of devotion, it would follow that those who are most apt for contemplation are most apt for devotion. Yet the contrary is to be noticed, for devotion is frequently found in men of simplicity and members of the female sex who are defective in contemplation. Therefore contemplation is not the proper cause of devotion.'

Had we not the answer of St. Thomas we might speculate what answer would be given by an age of intellectual giants without parallel save at the height of Greek philosophy. Something like heroic sanctity and truth is in the answer of the supreme genius of the thirteenth century. ' Science and anything else conducive to greatness, is to man an occasion of self-confidence so that he does not wholly surrender himself to God. The result is that suchlike things sometimes occasion a hindrance to devotion ; while in simple souls and women devotion abounds by repressing pride.

' If, however, a man perfectly submits to God his science or any other perfection, by this very fact his devotion is increased.' [2, 2ᵃᵉ, Qu. 82, Art. 3, ad 3.] The gentle apologetic for the man of humble science is a priceless heirloom from the thirteenth century. Yet, as scholarship is in its essence accuracy, St. Thomas is at pains to champion or at least to reassure those whose natural bent towards evil leads them to envy ' souls naturally Christian.' Thus he says :

' The natural inclination to a good of virtue is a kind of beginning of virtue ; but it is not perfect virtue. For the stronger this inclination is the more perilous may it prove to be, unless it is accompanied by right reason which rectifies the choice of fitting means towards the true end. Thus if a running horse be blind the faster it runs the more heavily will it fall, and the more grievously

H

will it be hurt. And consequently although moral virtue be not right reason, as Socrates held, yet not only is it according to right reason, in so far as it inclines man to that which is according to right reason as the Platonists maintained [Plato—*Menon* xli.]; but also it needs to be with right reason, as Aristotle declares.' [*Ethic.* vi. ; 1ᵃ, 2ᵃᵉ, Qu. 58, Art. 4, ad 3ᵐ.]

Even the casual reader of the *Summa* can hardly overlook this masterly synthesis of the three chief Greek schools of ethical thought on a fundamental problem of ethics. But the Christian student of asceticism will not fail to feel that to the sober wisdom of the great Christian thinker has been given some of the essential mercy of Him who was counted with the sinners and the publicans.

Another subject on which his mind had been working from his earliest teaching years, was that of attention in prayer. He had dealt with the subject when as a young professor he commented on the Sentences of Peter Lombard. This thought grew with his. years. Already in commenting on the first Epistle to the Corinthians he has developed the matter beyond any of his predecessors. But about two years. before his death he has reached the masterly synthesis which we find in the 2ᵃ, 2ᵃᵉ, Qu. 83, Art. 13.

A characteristically accurate observation is given a place in this commentary on the first Epistle to the Corinthians. He observes : ' Vix unum Pater noster possit homo dicere quin mens ad alia feratur.' [I. *Cor.* xiv., lect. 3.] ' A man can hardly say one Our Father without his mind wandering to something else.'

Here, again, he is on the side of the average Christian, when he says : ' There are three kinds of attention that can be brought to vocal prayer : one which attends to the words, lest we say them wrong ; another, which attends to the sense of the words ; and a third which attends to the end of prayer, namely, God and to the thing we are praying for. This last kind of attention is most necessary, and even simple folk (*idiotae*) are capable of it. Moreover this attention whereby the mind is fixed on God, is sometimes so strong that the mind forgets all other things, as Hugh of St. Victor states : *De Modo Orandi ii.* [2ª, 2ᵃᵉ, Qu. 83, Art. 13.]

Students of St. John of the Cross—especially of the *Ascent of Mount Carmel*—need hardly be reminded of the Spanish mystic's doctrine on the affections of the will. But they have probably not realised how heavy are his borrowings from St. Thomas' treatise on the *Passions*.

An acute French thinker of the middle nineteenth century had written : ' Quelle est donc en psychologie la part originale qui revient à saint Thomas ? Outre la rigeur de l'exposition que là, comme partout ailleurs, il ne doit qu'à lui-même ce qui, selon nous, lui appartient le plus clairement, c'est l'analyse profonde, minutieuse, fidèle des *passions*. . . . En géneral, le modele qu'il a devant les yeux est la nature de l'homme. Ainsi, on remarquera que les articles correspondants de la Somme de Theologie ne contiennent que peu de citations ; la connaissance du coeur humain y remplace l'erudition.

' La morale de saint Thomas est la partie de ses ouvrages qui passe pour être la plus remarquable.' [*La philosophie de saint Thomas d'Aquin.* Ch. Jourdain. Paris, 1858. Pp. 447, 448.]

But it is the Mystical rather than the Moral Theology of this masterly treatise on the Passions which is authenticated by the following anecdote told by the biographer of the Curé d'Ars. ' Nous lui avions souvent entendus dire que le coeur des saints était *liquide*. Nous avions eté frappé de cette ravissante et energique expression ; mais nous étions loin de soupçonner qu'elle êut une si grande précision theologique. C'est avec une surprise attendrie, au souvenir de notre bon saint, que nous avons trouvé, en feuilletant la Somme une question dans laquelle le Docteur angélique assigne à l'amour quatre effets immediats, dont le premier est *la liquefaction du coeur*.' [1ª, 2ᵃᵉ, Qu. 38, Art. 5.] [*Le Curé d'Ars. Vie de M. Jean-Baptiste*

Marie Vianney. Par l'Abbé Alfred Monnin. Paris, 1861.
P. 408.]

Any attempt to suggest the mystical yield of this
treatise by a few gatherings would be unpardonable were
it not all we can do in the time we can spend. Two such
selections from the Saint's heavy vintage must bring our
study to a close. St. Thomas ends a most painstaking
analysis of the difference between Love, Charity and
Dilection with the following doctrine : ' The reason why
some held that, even when applied to the will itself, the
word Love signifies something more god-like than Dilection,
was because Love denotes a passion, especially in so far
as it is in the sensitive appetite; whereas Dilection [1] presupposes the judgment of reason. But it is possible for
man to tend to God by Love, being as it were passively
drawn to Him, more than he can possibly be drawn thereto
by his reason, which pertains to the nature of Dilection.
And consequently Love is more god-like than Dilection.'
[1ª, 2ᵃᵉ, Qu. 26, Art. 3, ad 4.]

Our next gathering will be from a Question which by its
bare index would prove St. Thomas a Mystical writer of
first magnitude. The questions he asks and answers are
these.

1. Whether Union is an effect of Love ?
2. Whether mutual indwelling is an effect of Love ?
3. Whether ecstasy is an effect of Love ?
4. Whether zeal is an effect of Love ?
5. Whether Love is a passion that wounds the lover ?
6. Whether Love is cause of all that the lover does ?

The first article on Union and Love contains the following profound doctrine : ' Union has a threefold relation to
Love. There is a union which *causes* love ; and this is
substantial union as regards the love with which one
loves oneself ; while as regards the love wherewith one
loves other things it is the union of likeness.

' There is also a union which is *essentially* Love itself.
This union is according to a bond of affection and is likened

---

[1] Derived from *dis* and *eligere*, to choose.

to substantial union, inasmuch as the lover stands to the object of his love, as to himself if it be the love of friendship ;—as to something belonging to himself if it be the love of concupiscence.

'Again, there is a union which is the *effect* of Love. This is real union, which the lover seeks with the object of his love. Moreover this union is in keeping with the demands of love ; for as the Philosopher relates [*Politic ii.*], *Aristophanes stated that lovers would wish to be united both into one*, but since *this would result in either one or both being destroyed*, they seek a suitable and becoming union— to live together, speak together and be united in other like things. . . . . . Knowledge is perfected by the thing known being united, through its likeness, to the knower. But the effect of love is that the thing itself which is loved is in a way united to the lover. Consequently the union caused by love is closer than that which is caused by knowledge.' [1ª, 2ᵃᵉ, Qu. 28, Art. 1, ad 2, 3.

One last quotation may fitly end our endeavour to show St. Thomas as a supreme teacher of that Theology which is called Mystical, and therefore hidden, dark, detached. In dealing with the question whether the Fruits of the Holy Ghost are acts, he says : ' When the will is said to delight in a thing for its own sake, this may be understood in two ways. First, so that the expression *for the sake of* be taken to designate the final cause ; and in this way man delights in nothing for its own, except the last end. Secondly, so that it express the formal cause, and in this way a man may delight in anything that is delightful by reason of its form. . . . Accordingly we must say that man must delight in God for His own sake, as being his last end ; and in virtuous deeds, not as being his end, but for the sake of their inherent goodness which is delightful to the virtuous.' [1ª, 2ᵃᵉ, Qu. 70, Art. 1, ad 2.]

To this undaunted seeker after Truth, Goodness and Beauty, not even the soul's virtue was the soul's aim ; but God alone who was the soul's beginning, was the soul's last end.

St. Thomas
as an Interpreter of Holy Scripture

By Hugh Pope, O.P.

TO many minds the idea of any save the Ancient Fathers of the Church—and these with grave reservations,—and modern Commentators, being regarded as qualified interpreters of Scripture provokes a smile. That a Scholastic of the Middle Ages should be held up as an example of what a Biblical expositor should be seems little short of preposterous. Probably many would be inclined to say à *priori* of St. Thomas' Biblical work what was recently said of St. Ambrose[1] :—

'In his eyes it (the Bible) is really a species of sacred cypher. The plain, obvious meaning of any passage is never the whole of of what it is intended to mean to the Christian reader. Faith lives by the deeper meanings which can be disinterred, and the task of the Christian teacher is to lay these before his audience. To this task St. Ambrose brought an utterly uncritical mind, unhampered by any knowledge of Hebrew or by any considerations of historical perspective. He is like a man turning over an immense heap of variously shaped fragments. What the original design may have been does not concern him. He merely fits them together as his fancy prompts him into wholly unexpected patterns. . . . No doubt as to the value of the patterns which he formed seems ever to have crossed his mind.'

A similar treatment is often meted out to St. Thomas, the heir of all Patristic learning, the 'Light of the Church,' the 'Doctor Communis,' the 'Angelic Doctor' as he came to be called later. He is supposed to have been without any knowledge of Greek or Hebrew, to lack historical perspective, to view the Bible through theological

[1] *Journal of Theol. Studies*, July, 1915.

spectacles, to use texts regardless of their context, even regardless of their literal meaning, etc.

In the following pages we propose to try and discover to what extent St. Thomas was equipped for the task of commenting on the Bible.

In the Middle Ages it would have been idle to look for *Manuals of Biblical Introduction* such as we are accustomed to. But there did exist a Treatise which was widely read and from which St. Thomas quotes repeatedly, the *De Doctrina Christiana* of St. Augustine. In the first three Books Augustine lays down the principles which must necessarily guide a student of the Sacred Text. The famous Rules of the Donatist expositor, Tyconius, are analysed and approved by Augustine, and St. Thomas himself quotes them.[1] In the Fourth Book the natural transference is made from the study of the Bible to its exposition in the pulpit as food for men's souls.

St Augustine's Bible was of course the Old-Latin Bible translated from the Septuagint, to which version he constantly turns for illumination of the Latin text.[2] Hebrew he apparently did not know, though he was certainly acquainted with the Punic still spoken in Africa in his day.[3]

What Latin text, then, did St. Thomas use ? What Books constituted the Canon of the Bible in his time ? What knowledge—if any—had he of Hebrew and Greek ?

(i.) *His Latin Bible.*—We are not to look to St. Thomas for a discussion of the text or of principles of textual criticism. For first of all he is concerned with theology and is content to take the official text in use in the Church. Textual criticism is outside his province. Moreover, that work had already been done as far as was then possible, and as far as St. Thomas' requirements went. Early in the thirteenth century the newly-founded University of

---

[1] *Summa Theol.* IIIa. xv. i. *ad* 1m.

[2] *E.g. De Civ. Dei*, XV. xiii. ; *Tract* iii. 8, lxxxii. 1, lxxxiii. 2 *in Joann.* ; *Ep.* civ. 6, cxlix. 5, 8, &c.

[3] *E.g. Ep.* xl., xvii. 2, lxvi. 2, cviii. 14, ccix. 3 ; *Sermo* clxvii. 4, cclxxxviii. 3 ; *Tract.* xiv. 7, xv. 27 *in Joann.* ; *Haer.* lxxxvii. ; *Inchoata Expositio in Ep. ad Rom.* 13.

Paris agreed, for uniformity, to accept one particular Alcuinian recension of the Latin Bible as the basis for their lectures. Unfortunately it was a bad text; in its passage through the hands of many copyists it had suffered much. The action of the University, however, led to its multiplication. And the fact that it was divided up into chapters, either by Stephen Langton or by the Dominican Hugo à S. Caro, made it a popular text. At the same time its defects were well known, and various professors corrected it as occasion arose. These ' corrections ' were at first placed in the margin but later were published in separate books known as ' Correctories,' of which three hundred manuscript copies still survive. The ' Correctory' of the Sorbonne and that of Sens—known as the *Paris Correctory*—are the most famous. The framers of the *Paris Correctory* did not aim at recovering St. Jerome's Latin text, but rather at correcting the existing Vulgate text by the Hebrew and Greek originals. Thus Cardinal Hugo à S. Caro—who was mainly responsible for its production—says : ' In many books, especially the historical ones, we do not use the translation made by Jerome.' Yet Hugo's own Order was well aware of the defects of his Correctory ; thus in the General Chapter held by the Dominicans in 1236 it is laid down that ' all the Bibles in the Order are to be corrected according to the " correctory " of the (Dominican) Province of France ' ; but twenty years later the Chapter of 1256 rejected the Correctory of Sens as being an insufficient correction of the Bible of the University of Paris. There still exist three of the Correctories which belonged to the famous Dominican House of Studies at S. Jacques in Paris ; they probably date from the Chapter of 1256 when St. Thomas had just taken his degree as Master in theology and was at the height of his fame.

The tradition is that during his two years' imprisonment by his brothers, who endeavoured to make him give up the idea of becoming a Friar, St. Thomas learned the whole Vulgate Bible by heart. This story certainly receives full support from his writings.[1] The words of the Bible literally pour from him ; he seems to be able to recall any passage at will. Anyone can test this for himself if he will but examine the first six lectures in the Saint's *Commentary on Romans.* The lectures are brief, yet they contain no less than two hundred and eighty-three citations from the Bible ; he quotes fifty-three books, thirty-one from the Old Testament and twenty-two from the New. It is the same throughout his theological writings. Unquestionably he often quotes from memory, though lapses are rare. Many of his variations from the Tridentine Vulgate are probably due to his use of a different text; but they need not detain us here.[2] What does concern us is the minute attention he always pays to the actual letter of the text and his insistence on its precision and its authority.[3] It is true that in doing this he is not urging the claims of the Latin text over the originals ; he is simply insisting on the authority of the text of Scripture which he regards as sufficiently guaranteed for us in the Vulgate. At the same time St. Thomas is not blind to the existence of textual difficulties. Thus he quotes Origen on Ephes. i. 5 and is well aware of his difference in the reading ;[4] though at another time, while quoting him on the eclipse at the death of Christ, he pays no attention to Origen's divergent text.[5] For St. Thomas such details are secondary matters.

(ii.) St. Thomas' *Canon of Scripture.*—(*a*) About the Deutero-canonical Books, *i.e. Tobias, Judith, Wisdom, Ecclesiasticus, Baruch* and the *Epistle of Jeremias, I.-II. Maccabees,* St. Thomas has no doubt whatever ; he quotes

---

[1] Thus apropos of the words *odio habebis inimicum tuum* in Matt. v. 43, he remarks ' in toto veteri Testamento non inveniuntur,' *De Caritate,* viii. *ad* 5tm.

[2] As instances of curious readings note *miracula* for *mirabilia* in Ps. lxxi. 18, *De Potentia* VI. iv., *Sed contra* ; also the curious text of Exod. xxii. 24 (25) and Ecclus. xxix. 10 in *De Malo,* xiii. 4, *Sed contra* and *ad* 2dm. ; his reading *cupio dissolvi* instead of *desiderium habens dissolvi* in Phil. i. 23, *Contra Errores Graecorum,* ix. ; his reading *certe* for *celte* in Job xix., though in his Commentary on *Job* he has *celte,* as in the Tridentine Vulgate.

[3] *E.g. De Veritate,* II. xi. *ad* 1m. ; *De Potentia,* iv. 1 *ad* 17m. ; and 2.

[4] *Summa Theol.* IIIa. xxiv. 1 *ad* 3m.

[5] *Ibid.* xliv. 2 *ad* 2dm. ; *cf.* Origen, *Series in Matt.* 134 ; *P. G.* XIII. 1783.

them incessantly and as of equal authority with the Books found in the Hebrew Canon. Thus nine of the twelve chapters of *Tobias* are quoted in the *Summa Theologica* alone, and each chapter many times over ; the same holds good for *Judith*, of which eleven out of sixteen chapters are quoted, and repeatedly, in the *Summa* ; so too eleven out of the nineteen chapters of *Wisdom* are quoted. The *Books of Maccabees* naturally do not lend themselves to quotation in a purely theological treatise, yet they are cited as authorities now and again. The only doubt that ever seems to be expressed concerns *Ecclesiasticus*. St. Thomas quotes Ecclus. xlvi. 23 with regard to the raising of Samuel by the witch of Endor : *And after this he slept and he made known to the king the end of his life ;* but St. Thomas adds : ' It may also be said that that apparition was brought about by evil spirits ; that is if the authority of *Ecclesiasticus* is not admitted on the ground that the Hebrews do not reckon it among the Canonical Scriptures.' It is hardly pertinent to say that he has in view controversy with Jews, who would of course not accept the authority of *Ecclesiasticus*, for he is here discussing a purely speculative question : whether souls separated from the body know what is being done here below ? Probably, too, most Jews would accept the authority of Ben Sirach. But as a matter of fact St. Thomas is here simply quoting St. Augustine, who says that if any Jew repudiates the authority of *Ecclesiasticus* on the ground that it is not in the Hebrew Canon he can be retorted on by quoting the case of Moses, of whose death we know from *Deuteronomy*—certainly in the Hebrew Canon—and who yet appeared at the Transfiguration.[1]

The books commonly known as *III.-IV. Esdras* were much in use amongst the Fathers of the Church, and out of respect for the frequent use they made of them, the Council of Trent laid down after much discussion [2] that these two Books should be preserved in the edition of the

---

[1] *De Cura Mortuorum*, xv. ; *P. L.* XL. 606.
[2] See the *Diaria Tridentina*, Vol. I. pp. 31, 521, 522, 684 for the discussion.

Vulgate which the Council had ordered to be prepared. Now St. Thomas quotes these Books, *III.-IV. Esdras*, several times. Sometimes he does so without any comment as to their authenticity;[1] at other times he writes : ' in Apocryphis Esdrae . . .'[2] We cannot—on the ground that in his early work, the *Commentary on the Sentences*, he quotes them without any *caveat*—argue that he changed his mind, or that he only learned later that these Books were apocryphal, for he does the same in his latest work, the *Summa Theologica*. Certainly he never uses them as authorities, that is in that portion of his Articles which is termed the ' Sed contra ' wherein, previous to his reasoned discussion on the point at issue, he sets down some authority for the view he is going to uphold.

Whether the same is to be said of his solitary (as far as is known to us) citation of the *Prayer of Manasses*,[3] is not clear. In the printed editions the citation is preceded by the words ' Hence it is said (*II. Paralip. ult. in oratione Manasses, ante lib. tertium Esdrae*).' But whose are the brackets ? It seems certain that they are simply due to an editor, since the *Prayer of Manasses* and *III.-IV. Esdras* were presumably only grouped together by the editors of the Tridentine Vulgate.[4] If that is so, then he is apparently quoting without any reservation a writing which was certainly not canonical.

(*b*)—As for the well-known Apocrypha, whether of the Old or the New Testament, St. Thomas is remarkably silent about them. He never—so far as we are aware—quotes even the *Shepherd* of Hermas. In fact, as far as we can discover, the only two apocryphal works he ever cites are *De Ortu Salvatoris* and *De Infantia Salvatoris*,[5] both of which, in his answer to the difficulty suggested by passages from them, he repudiates as apocryphal. An

---

[1] Comment. on the *Prologue* to the *Sentences* ; *Summa Theol.* 2da. 2dae. cxlv. 4 *ad* 2 dm.

[2] *Summa Theol.* Ia. x. 6 *ad* 1m. 2da. 2dae. xxxiv. 1 *ad* 1m.

[3] *Summa Theol.* IIIa. lxxxiv..10.

[4] The Complutensian Polyglott has the *Prayer of Manasses* in Latin across the whole page devoted to the Hebrew, Greek, and Latin text of *Chronicles*.

[5] *Summa Theol.* IIIa. xxxv. 6 *ad* 3m. and xxxvi. 4 *ad* 3m.

interesting example of his method of using a notoriously
apocryphal work is furnished by his citations from the
Clementines. He once at least quotes the *Itinerarium
Clementis* in a difficulty which he proposes ; in his answer
he makes no reference to its authenticity.[1] But in another
place, where he again quotes it as furnishing an argument
against his doctrine, he immediately adds : ' Yet this
book is proscribed in the *Decretals, dist.* 15 *cap.* " *Sancta
Romana Ecclesia.*" '[2]

(iii.) St. Thomas' *acquaintance with the Septuagint version.*
—When discussing the meaning of the expression *And the
earth was void and empty,* ' inanus et vacua,' the ' chaos '
of Gen. i. 2, St. Thomas notes that ' secundum aliam
litteram,' that is ' according to another interpretation,'
this is given as ' invisibilis et incomposita ' ;[3] on at least
three occasions does he draw attention to this, and once
he expressly mentions that this is ' secundum litteram
Septuaginta.'[4] He may simply have known this from
St. Augustine who in his various expositions of *Genesis*
always so reads it.[5] But as there are certain other places
where St. Thomas shews an acquaintance with the Septuagint readings it seems probable that his knowledge of
this reading in *Genesis* was due as much to his own acquaintance with the Septuagint as to his familiarity with
St. Augustine. Thus he refers to St. Paul's quotation[6]
of Habacuc[7] *the just man liveth by faith,* and remarks
' This is taken from the Septuagint text, but in our version
(the Vulgate), which is in accordance with the Hebrew
truth, we have ' the just man shall live by *his* faith.' This
will not of course prove that he actually looked up the
Septuagint on the passage ; he may simply have taken
it on hearsay. But when we find him quoting the Septuagint text of *Nahum*[8] : *He* (God) *shall not judge twice in*

---

[1] *De Malo,* X. ii., *Sed contra* 2.
[2] *Summa Theol.* Ia. cxvii. 4, 2nd difficulty.
[3] *Summa Theol.* Ia. lxvi. i. 1.
[4] *De Potentia,* iv. 1 *ad* 7m. ; *cf. De Spiritualibus Creaturis,* i. *ad* 4m.
[5] *E.g. De Genesi ad litt.* I. i. (3).
[6] Rom. i. 17. *Lectio* vi. on Rom. i.
[7] Hab. ii. 4. [8] Nahum i. 9. *Summa Theol.* IIIa. lix. 5, 2nd difficulty.

tribulation, a reading which has no affinity whatever with our Vulgate text, and when again we find him pointing out that according to the Septuagint the work of Creation was completed on the sixth day and not on the seventh—as in our version,[1] it seems difficult to maintain that St. Thomas' knowledge of this version was simply second-hand.

Much the same must be said of St. Thomas' familiarity with the *Greek text of the New Testament.* Thus apropos of St. Luke's description of the forty days following upon the Resurrection : *He shewed Himself . . . . by many proofs* (in multis argumentis) *for forty days appearing,*[2] St. Thomas explains this as meaning that ' By certain evident signs He shewed that He had truly risen ; ' hence in the Greek, where we have *in multis argumentis,* τεκμήριον is given instead of ' *argumentis.*' [3]   Similarly, apropos of the difficulty arising from St. Mark's statement that *it was the third hour when they crucified Him*—instead of the sixth,[4] the comment is ' Some say that this divergence arose from the mistake of a Greek copyist ; for with the Greeks the figures representing three and six are very similar.'[5]   St. Thomas' derivations have often provoked a smile ; he owed them as a rule to St. Isidore and gives them for what they are worth ; yet he gives correctly the derivation of ἀνάθεμα, *anathema.*[6]   Similarly in *Ecclesiasticus*[7] we are told that *Wisdom is according to her name,* and the current punning derivation was ' sapientia est sapida scientia.' Now St. Thomas uses this as an argument against a point of doctrine he is upholding; but he remarks, ' It is a question whether that really is the meaning of that passage ; it hardly seems to be so since it is simply based on the Latin word *sapientia* and has no relation to the word in Greek.' [8]   Lastly, he knows that the Greek

[1] *Summa Theol.* lxxiii. i. *ad* 2m.
[2] Acts i. 3.
[3] *Summa Theol.* IIIa. lv. 5.   The printed text has τεκμήριον for τεκμηρίοις.
[4] Mark xv. 25.
[5] *Summa Theol.* xlvi. 9 *ad* 2m.
[6] *Lect.* i. on Rom. ix.   [7] vi. 43.
[8] *Summa Theol.* 2da. 2dae. xlv. 2 *ad* 2m.

text does not support the Vulgate *Sic eum volo manere* in St. John xxi.[1]

Greek, then, was no sealed book to St. Thomas. It must be remembered that he was a Neapolitan, that consequently he lived almost in Magna Graecia where Greek was the common medium during a very long period.[2] At the same time it seems clear that Greek was not a familiar vehicle for his thoughts. One can have little doubt that he could have at least spelled out laboriously the writings of the Greek Fathers, but he naturally preferred to have them translated for him,[3] as had been the case with the Aristotle he used.[4]

It is amusing to find Tholuck, in a dissertation he published in 1842,[5] demolishing in a scant eleven lines the notion that St. Thomas knew Greek! He goes by the facts that some of his derivations are bizarre, and also that he knew the Greek Fathers in a Latin dress.

All doubts about St. Thomas' knowledge of Greek should however be effectively dispelled when we reflect on the minuteness of his study of the text of Aristotle. A perusal of one of his most profound treatises, *De Unitate Intellectus*, will suffice to shew that he used Aristotle in Greek perhaps quite as freely as in Latin. But as he was writing in Latin and for people who habitually used Latin, he naturally preferred to have a good translation.[6] Two instances will suffice : apropos of a disputed passage of Aristotle which Averroes had wrested to his own purposes, St. Thomas says : ' This he (Aristotle) proves at once, and

[1] *Lect. v. in Joann.* ; Just as he knows that *Salome* is not the name of a man ' ut etiam in Graeco apparet,' *Lect.* v. on Gal. i.

[2] See K. Lake, *Greek Monasteries in Southern Italy*, *J.T.S.* 1903-4.

[3] As he tells us expressly in the Dedicatory Epistle to his *Catena Aurea* on St. Mark ; though it should be noted that he does not say that this was because he could not read them in Greek, but because he was writing in Latin. After all it is hard to see how he could have indicated the passages he wanted translated unless he himself could have read them in the original.

[4] By the two Dominicans, Henry of Brabant and William of Moerbeke.

[5] *Disputatio de Thoma Aquinate atque Abelardo interpretibus Novi Testamenti*, 1842. A similar treatise by Bernardus Guyardus *Utrum S. Thomas calluerit linguam Graecam ?* appeared in 1672, but we have not seen it.

[6] Note that Tocco in his *Vita*, iv. 18 says that being dissatisfied with existing translations of Aristotle, St. Thomas had a fresh translation made for him.

the text runs as follows in Greek'; he then gives the literal translation of the Greek, a translation which compares favourably with more recent ones.[1]   A little farther on in the same treatise he remarks ' that Aristotle solved these questions can be deduced with certainty from those Books which it is clear that he wrote on *Separated Substances*, as he says in the opening of his Twelfth Book on *Metaphysics*, which Books, fourteen in number, we have seen though not as yet translated into our language.'

(iv.) St. Thomas' *knowledge of Hebrew.*—It is a commonplace among modern writers that the Fathers and the Scholastics knew no Hebrew.   St. Jerome is always regarded as an exception that proves the rule.   But is it true ?   It would seem that the ideas held by the Fathers and by us moderns on the subject of knowledge of a language differ considerably.   We are all familiar with the young lady whose French was learned at Stratford at Bow, and who could say with difficulty ' ce n'est que le premier pas qui coute,' but who would be indignant if told that she did not really know French.   Because St. Augustine says that as a boy he had no particular liking for Greek[2] it is always supposed that he did not know any.   But the person who says that Augustine did not know Greek—and know it well—does not know his Augustine ![3]   If we remember aright St. Gregory the Great says somewhere that he does not know Greek ; yet he was the representative of the Roman court at Constantinople for a considerable time.   The truth is that when the Fathers spoke of knowing a language, they meant possessing it as a ready tool.   St. Jerome shews us this when he lets us see incidentally that he not only read but spoke Hebrew : ' As you know,' he writes to Marcella, ' I am busy reading Hebrew, and my Latin is getting rusty ; so much so that even when speaking I produce certain strident sounds which are certainly not Latin.'[4]

[1] See Gardeil, O.P. *Rev. Thomiste*, May, 1904 to June, 1905, articles to which our attention was only called after these pages had been written.
[2] *Contra Litteras Petiliani*, ii. 91.
[3] See for example *Contra Julianum*, I. 26, *P.L.* xliv. 658.   [4] *Ep.* xxix. 7.

To maintain the thesis that St. Thomas was a species of
Rabbi would be absurd.   But it would be no less absurd
to maintain that he knew no Hebrew.   We have got to rid
our minds of the notion that a knowledge of Hebrew only
came in with the Reformation.   One has only to reflect
on the preponderating part the Jews played in mediaeval
history to realise how wide of the truth such an idea would
be.   If Hebrew had not been at that period a language
fairly easily learned, Roger Bacon would never have dared
to boast that he would teach anyone Hebrew in three
days ! [1]   As a matter of fact St. Thomas betrays no
acquaintance with Hebrew ; as far as we are aware the
only references he makes to the language are his allusion to
a statement of St. Chrysostom's that in Hebrew the word
for ' heaven ' is in the plural,[2] and here he is wrong since
it is a dual; also his remark that the Hebrew language
has no letter *P*,[3] which is really true, though it seems to
shew that he had never heard of the mystic word *Begad-
kephath* !

He is well aware however that *Lamentations* is a species
of acrostic and that the verses follow the order of the
letters of the Hebrew Alphabet ; this is of course a trifling
detail and proves nothing for his knowledge of Hebrew.
But on one occasion he quotes St. Jerome's Gloss. on
Gen. vi., ' verbum Hebraicum אלהים utriusque numeri
est : Deum enim et Deos significat,' and the Hebrew
equivalent is given ; though whether this is due to later
editors or to St. Thomas himself we are not competent to
say.

[1] *Opus Minus*, p. 330 ; *Opus Tertium*, I. 94, *cap.* xxv.
[2] *Summa Theol.* Ia. lxviii. 4.   [3] *Lect.* i. on Rom. i.

B

His Idea of the Authority of the Bible

FOR St. Thomas the authority of Scripture is absolute. 'The authority of Scripture is sufficient' is often his answer to a difficulty which he is going however to try and unravel by the light of reason.[1] Thus when proving that Mary was the Mother of God, he puts the difficulty that 'nothing is to be held touching the Divine Mysteries save on the authority of Scripture, and that nowhere in Scripture is she called the Mother of God but only of Christ'; the principle is sound, he acknowledges, but its application false.[2] So, too, he rejects Origen's notions on the creation of corporeal matter on the ground that 'it is opposed to Scripture.'[3] 'The sole rule of faith,' he says, 'is the Canonic Scriptures';[4] and once more, 'Faith holds to all the articles of faith because of one principle (medium), viz. the primal truth set before us in the Scriptures according to the teaching of the Church, which has sound understanding of them.'[5] And again :

'The formal object of faith is the primal truth as made known to us in Sacred Scripture and in the teaching of the Church which proceeds from the primal truth. Consequently whoso does not adhere—as to an infallible and Divine rule—to the Church's teaching, which proceeds from the primal truth made known to us in the Scriptures, has not the habit of faith but holds the truths of faith on some other principle than faith ; we have a parallel when a person holds a conclusion without knowing the premises that led up to it, it is clear that such a person has not got knowledge but only opinion.'[6]

---

[1] E.g. Summa Theol. Ia. lxx. 1, Sed contra.
[2] Ibid. IIIa. xxxv. 4, 1st obj.   [3] Ibid. Ia. lxv. 2.
[4] Lectio vi. in Joann. xxi.   [5] Summa Theol. 2da. 2dae. v. 3 ad 2m.
[6] Ibid. in the body of the Article.

Similarly when refuting the Manichees, who held that Christ's body was not real, he is content to answer : ' This idea destroys the authority of Scripture. For since "the appearance of flesh" is not flesh, any more than the likeness of walking is walking, Scripture lies when saying *And the Word was made flesh.* . . . But if we detract from the authority of Holy Scripture in the slightest degree, then nothing can be positively certain in our faith which rests on Holy Scripture.' Nor will he tolerate the evasion that since Scripture narrates things which appeared to be as though they really were such, and that consequently Scripture would not lie in the above case : ' although likenesses of things are sometimes spoken of as though they were the things themselves, yet it is quite alien to Scripture to present the whole account of some event in such an equivocal fashion that the real truth of the matter cannot be gathered from other passages of Scripture ; for this would serve rather for man's deception than for his instruction. . . . Moreover the entire Gospel-narrative would be poetical and a fairy story if it told of mere appearances as though they were sober fact.' [1]

St. Thomas even extends the authority of Scripture to such scientific truths as belong to faith and morals. Thus he asks 'whether Prophecy is concerned with knowable conclusions ? ' [2] It should be noted that under the heading ' Prophecy ' he groups all Divine manifestations, revelation as well as inspiration.[3] He answers his question in the affirmative :

' We only believe the Prophets in so far as they are inspired by the spirit of prophecy. But we have to give the assent of faith to what is written in the prophetical books, even when their statements are concerned with scientific conclusions, as for example *He established the earth above the waters,* [4] or similar statements. Consequently the spirit of prophecy inspires the Prophets even regarding the conclusions of the sciences.' He proceeds to point

[1] *Contra Gentes*, IV. xxix.
[2] *De Veritate*, XII. 2.
[3] *Summa Theol.* 2da. 2dae. clxxi.-clxxiv., esp. clxxiii. 2.
[4] Ps. cxxxv. (cxxxvi.) 6.

out that since prophecy is simply for the sake of man's salvation, 'all those things which can help our salvation can be the subject-matter of prophecy, whether they are past, or future, or eternal, or necessary truths or contingent ones. . . . And by "neces-sary for salvation" I mean whether necessary for our instruction in the faith or for the formation of our moral character. Now many things which can be demonstrated by the sciences can be useful to this end, as for example the incorruptible nature of the intellect and those marvels in the created world which compel us to admire the wisdom and power of God; consequently we find such things mentioned in Holy Scripture.'

He then goes on to shew, however, that such truths are not the primary object of prophecy, though they do come under it.

Again :—

'Disciples can without difficulty take either side they please when Doctors of Scripture differ—provided their opinions do not conflict with the faith or sound morals. . . . As Augustine says : "Each one must consult the Rule of Faith which he has received from the plainer passages of Scripture and from the authority of the Church." [1] Whosoever, then, assents to the opinions of any teacher whatsoever when these conflict with the patent testimony of Scripture or with what is commonly held on the Church's authority, cannot be held excused from a vicious error.' [2]

Similarly, when opening his treatise on the Days of Creation he bases himself on St. Augustine's dictum that :

'In these questions two things have to be observed : first that the truth of Scripture must be preserved inviolate ; secondly that, since Scripture admits of different explanations, no one should so tenaciously adhere to his own view that—even when it has been proved to be false—he should still affirm it ; lest un-believers hence be led to scoff at the Scriptures and so the road to faith be closed to them.' [3]

[1] *Doctrina Christiana*, III. 2.   [2] *Quodl.* III. iv. 10.
[3] *Summa Theol.* Ia. lxviii. 1.

C

His Principles of Biblical Interpretation

(*a*) *Prophecy.*—' The whole purpose of Scripture,' St. Thomas says, ' is the knitting of man's soul to God, the Holy and the Supreme. . . . But we must note that there is this difference between Sacred Scripture and other sciences, that these latter emanate from human reason, while Scripture is due to the impulse of Divine inspiration.'[1] Those who receive such inspiration are termed ' Prophets ' : ' The Prophets of God,' he says, ' are those who through the ministry of Angels, as Denis says, receive from God an illumination concerning things future. Hence Cassiodorus says : " Prophecy is a divine inspiration declaring events with unshakable truth." ' Prophets, then, are inspired ; moreover they are ' sent of God ' and they bear witness to God. For their task they have a dignity that is all their own, but for its full exercise ' they must also have fraternal charity and kindly compassion.'[2]

Now the key to St. Thomas' exegesis and his use of Scripture in general lies in his conception of revelation and inspiration. For these he considers as subdivisions of the gift of Prophecy, which is one of the *gratiae gratis datae*, or gifts bestowed for the profit of others than their recipients. 'All the gratuitous graces which are concerned with knowledge may be grouped under Prophecy ' he says.[3] This gift of ' prophecy ' is not a permanent habit but a transiently communicated light ;[4] nor is it solely concerned with future things, though these are more particularly its object ; it may extend to all knowledge—whether of the past, the present or the future—which is beyond the natural ken of the human mind.[5] Since the recipients of

---

[1] *Proemium in Psalterium.*   [2] *Proemium in Comment. in Jerem.*
[3] *Prologue* to *Summa Theologica*, 2da. 2dae. clxxi.
[4] *Ibid.* clxxi. 2.   [5] *Ibid.* 3.

this gift do not see the essence of God but only a partial reflexion of it—seeing, as it were, ‘ in the mirror of eternity ’ [1]—their knowledge is not co-extensive with all truth, but precisely and only with that portion of truth which is divinely communicated to them.[2] Moreover there are degrees in a man’s certitude regarding the source of the knowledge he has thus received ; he may have an express revelation, he may only have what may be termed a prophetic instinct [3] ‘ such as human minds unconsciously experience,’ to use St. Augustine’s phrase.[4] What they do thus divinely know, however, cannot be false in any sense intended by the sacred writers,[5] yet all depends entirely on what precisely was revealed to them. They may, for instance, be shewn a future event as actually present—as indeed it is to God ; and then this revelation is absolutely true. On the other hand they may be shewn the relationship subsisting between cause and effect, without however learning whether according to the decrees of Providence those causes are actually destined to produce that effect. This is the key to all comminative prophecies, e.g. the illness of Ezechias should have led to his death, the sin of Ninive to its destruction.[6]

Again, prophecy is not divination nor mere conjecture—however well founded ; [7] nor indeed is any natural disposition a pre-requisite to it,[8] not even a virtuous life.[9]

Prophecy is, as St. Thomas laid down at the outset, a gift which has for its object the communication of some knowledge. Now knowledge implies two factors : reception of a truth and judgment upon it. A human teacher can supply men with truths but cannot interiorly illumine his disciple’s judgment. Yet such illumination, as being the final factor in knowledge, must needs be the principal feature in prophecy. Hence a mere dream—even if sent from God—as in the cases of Pharaoh [10] and Nebuchonosor [11]

---

[1] Summa Theol., 2da. 2dae. clxxiii. 1. De Potentia, iv. 2. ad 27m.
[2] Summa Theol., clxxi. 4.   [3] clxxi. 5.
[4] De Gen. ad Litt. ii. 17 (37), P.L. XXXIV. 278.
[5] Summa Theol. 2da. 2dae. clxxi. 6.   [6] Ib. clxxi. 6 ad 2dm.
[7] Ib. clxxii. 1.   [8] Ib. 3.   [9] Ib. 4.   [10] Gen. xli.   [11] Dan. ii.

cannot be termed 'prophecy.' On the other hand a person who receives from God a divine illumination touching those very dreams—as was the case with Joseph and Daniel—is most truly a prophet. And, as is expressly laid down by St. Augustine : ' He is especially a prophet who excells in both these things : who sees in spirit images significative of corporeal things and also understands them through the vivacity of his intellect.' [1]

(b) *Inspiration.*—Now this divine illumination of the judgment, which is the essential factor in knowledge but which is not a revelation, though it may accompany such revelation and make it intelligible to the recipient, is for St. Thomas the essential thing in inspiration. It may be accompanied by a divine impulse to the will to speak, as in the case of Joseph. It may be accompanied by an impulse to commit to writing what may have been received either in a purely natural way—as for instance by study or by hearing—or in a supernatural way, that is by Divine revelation. This was the case with Daniel, who learned from God what the king had dreamed and simultaneously received an illumination of his judgment so that he understood divinely what that dream meant, while he was further impelled to commit the story to writing.

Now all these things are grouped under the heading ' Prophecy,' which is a glimpse into the mirror of eternity, a partial view of the reflected mind of God. Consequently in no aspect can it be false. Hence, too, those who speak under such a divine impulse are absolutely correct; similarly those who write under it are absolutely correct, whether they are writing about what they have learned in a natural fashion or about what they have learned from God. In both cases the essential and primary feature of divine knowledge, *viz.* a divinely illumined judgment, is divinely bestowed upon them.[2]

---

[1] *De Gen. ad litt.* XII. ix. (20), *P.L.* XXXIV. 461.
[2] *Summa Theol.* 2da. 2dae. clxxiii. 2.   The same doctrine is given again and again, *e.g. Lect.* ii. on Rom. xii.; *Lect.* i. on I. Cor. xiii.; *Lect.* ii. on I. *Cor.* xi. ; *Lect.* i. on I. Cor. xiv.; *Lect.* vi. on II. Cor. xii.   *De Potentia,* IV. ii. 27 ; *De Veritate*, XII. throughout.

But several problems here emerge : what precisely
was shewn to the Prophets ' in the mirror of eternity ' ?
If God moves the human will to any act, does not the
man so moved become a merely mechanical instrument ?
Does the illumination of the writer's or speaker's judgment override his natural tendencies ?

(c) *Instrumental Causality.*—With regard to the first
question : no created mind can adequately grasp a revealed
truth. The Prophets are shewn sufficient for them to have
material whereon to form a judgment, and they are shewn
precisely what God wills, and no more. When Isaias,
for example, foretold the Virgin-birth of Christ, he knew
the fact for certain, but how much did he grasp of its
circumstances ?   Had he any idea when it would come
to pass ?   And if the human mind can only inadequately
apprehend a divine truth, still less can the human tongue
express adequately what the mind has grasped. There
must always be a gulf between the divine knowledge and
the partial glimpse of it afforded to the Prophet ; there
must be another gulf between his knowledge and his
expression of it.

The second and third questions may be grouped together.
When we use instruments we use them according to their
nature ; in other words we do not do violence to them.
Moreover we use instruments precisely because of certain
inherent qualities they possess ; if they had them not we
should not use them. Further, from an instrument
properly applied there flows an effect which it is utterly
beyond the power of the instrument to produce. My
razor *cuts* ; it does not *shave*. Shaving is a result flowing
from the combined action of my brain and my wrist,
as well as of the razor. Yet the whole effect flows from
both myself and the razor. If the razor is a poor one the
effect is bad ; if it is in good condition and yet only poor
results are achieved, this is due to my lack of skill. If on
the other hand my skill were such that I could not only
use a razor but could actually make one, and was in a
position to choose the finest steel and temper it precisely

for my own purposes, then I should stand a good chance of
securing results as nearly perfect as possible.

If it were possible to go still further and secure an instrument which was actually part of myself it would then act,
as it were, spontaneously, and would do exactly what I
want and in the way I want. We have an instance of
this in the human hand. We have the most perfect
instance of all in the Sacred Humanity assumed by the
Son of God as the instrument whereby He would work out
our Redemption. Yet even that Humanity is finite and
cannot adequately express the mind of the Son of God Who
wielded it as an instrument.

St. Thomas himself acknowledges that this doctrine is
difficult to grasp : ' To some it seems hard,' he says, ' to
understand how natural effects can be attributed to God
and to a natural agent. Yet the difficulties alleged are
not real when we consider the following principles :

' In every agent we have to consider two things : the thing that
acts and the power by which it acts—fire, for instance, warms by
heat. Now the power of an inferior agent depends on the power
of the superior agent, in that the latter either actually bestows on
the inferior the power by which the latter acts, or preserves that
power, or applies it so that it acts. Thus a workman applies an
instrument for the production of its own proper effect, yet he does
not confer on that instrument the power whereby it acts, nor
does he preserve that power in being ; he merely sets it in motion.

' Consequently the action of an inferior agent not only flows
from it by its own proper power but by the power of all the
preceding agents ; for it acts in virtue of them all. And just as
the lowest instrument in the scale is found to be immediately
active, so too the power of the first agent in the series is found to
be immediately active for the production of its effect. For the
power of the lowest agent is not capable of producing this effect
of itself but only in virtue of the agent immediately above it in
the scale. So too the power of this latter acts in virtue of the
power of the one above it. Thus the power of the supreme agent
in the series is found to be of itself productive of the effect as
though it were its immediate cause. This is evident in the
principles of demonstrations where the first are immediate in
effect.

' Consequently, just as there is nothing incongruous in the
notion that one action should flow from a particular agent and its

power, so there is nothing incongruous in the idea that one and the same effect should be produced by an inferior agent and by God, immediately by both, though in different ways.' [1]

As for the difficulty that this seems to make a man a mere mechanical instrument :

' That argument is based on the notion of an instrument whose function it is to be acted on, not to act. But man is not an instrument of that sort ; he is so acted on by the Holy Spirit that he himself also acts—since he has free will.' [2]

In the same sense he quotes, apropos of the Gifts of the Holy Spirit, the words of Aristotle :

' Those who are moved by a divine instinct do not need to take counsel of their reason but must follow their interior instinct, since they are moved by a better principle,' better, namely, than human reason. [3]

This doctrine touching the real nature of instrumental action is stated many times by St. Thomas ; it is a fundamental principle of his philosophy and therefore of his theology. But he sets it out with peculiar insistence when treating of another gratuitous grace, namely the gift of working miracles. Men and Angels, he says,

' Act as the instruments of the Divine power . . . not indeed as though this power resided in them habitually . . . rather is this power of co-operation with God in working miracles comparable to the action of imperfect " forms " which are only there so long as the principal agent is present, just as the light is in the air, and movement in an instrument. . . . It is the same with the grace of Prophecy, which is bestowed for the sake of supernatural knowledge ; by its means the Prophet cannot prophesy when he likes but only when the spirit of prophecy touches his heart.' [4]

That God can, and of necessity does, move the human will to · its acts is another fundamental principle with St. Thomas ; the whole of his doctrine on Grace and Predestination depends on it. The *locus classicus* for this doctrine is of course the following :

[1] *Contra Gentes*, III. lxx.
[2] *Summa Theol.* Ia, 2dae, lxviii. iii. *ad* 2m.
[3] *Ibid.* Ia. IIae. lxviii. 1.
[4] *De Potentia*, VI. iv.

' It is no part of Divine Providence to destroy, but to preserve the nature of things. Hence He moves all things according to their condition, so that from necessary causes there follow—owing to the Divine motion—necessary effects, and from contingent causes follow contingent effects. Since, then, the will is an active principle not of its nature determined to one of two alternatives, God so moves it as not to determine it of necessity to one of these, but its movement remains contingent and not necessary.' [1]

To this we may add :

' The First Cause is more potent in the production of an effect than the second ; consequently, whatever perfection is in that effect, it is to be referred principally to the First Cause ; while whatever defect is there is referable to the second cause, which does not act with such efficacy as the First Cause.' [2]

And again :

' God works perfectly as the First Cause ; yet the operation of nature as a secondary cause is requisite.   None the less God could produce nature's effects without the intervention of nature ; He wishes, however, to act through the medium of nature for the preservation of harmony in things.' [3]

(d) *The Different ' Senses ' of Scripture.*—The application of the foregoing to our question may not seem clear at first sight. But we shall see that the principles invoked are fundamental. When St. Thomas is discussing the possibility of Scripture possessing a spiritual as well as a literal sense he puts this difficulty : ' No meaning drawn from the wording of Scripture other than what the writer meant can be termed its real meaning, for the author of any portion of Scripture could only have had one meaning in mind since, as the Philosopher says : "No one can mean several things at once." ' His reply is significant :

' I reply that the principal Author of Holy Scripture is the Holy Spirit, Who in any one expression of Scripture meant far more than any expositor can expound or discover. At the same time there is nothing repugnant in the notion that man, who is the instrumental cause of Holy Scripture, should in one expression mean several things. For the Prophets, as St. Jerome says on *Osee,* so spoke of present facts as to intend thereby to signify

[1] *Summa Theol.* Ia, 2ae, X. iv.   [2] *De Potentia,* III. vii. *ad* 15m.
[3] *Ibid. ad* 16m.

future things. Consequently it is not impossible to mean several things at once, when, that is, one is a figure of another.' [1]

The point immediately concerning us is that here St. Thomas positively declares that the inspired writers are the instrumental causes which God applies. When, then, God inspires—that is illumines a man's judgment, on certain things which have been either divinely told him or acquired in a natural fashion, and at the same time moves him to commit those facts, on which his judgment has thus been divinely illumined, to writing—He is using men as His instruments. That is, He is using them precisely because of certain qualities they possess and in accordance with those qualities. He is doing no violence to natures which He has Himself created. And these same qualities they owe to Him. Why did He bestow them? Why, for example, did He make Isaias a poet, a diplomat if you will, a courtier, a member of the royal stock? Why did He make Osee a farmer with the mind and outlook of a farmer? Surely because He was doing what we cannot do save inadequately, *viz.* creating from eternity instruments whom, when the due time came, He would move and apply for the production of a certain work which He had, also from eternity, designed to produce? When that time came He illumined the judgment of a poet or a farmer, as the case may be, precisely because he was such; and he was such because from eternity God planned him to be such for the production of that particular Book of the Bible. Still further: He moves the will of each according to the nature He has given them. He has nothing to change or correct. Nothing in their work will require His revision. If the writer's nature is artistic the result will be a word-picture, as in the case of St. Luke's *Gospel*: if he is a Levite with certain prepossessions, the result—and it is God's result—will be *Chronicles*.

Now it will be clear that in all this two minds are at work: the Mind of God and the mind of the human instrument He employs. Each will be working to the

[1] *Quodl.* VII. 14 *ad* 5m.

fullness of its capacity, the one as applying, the other as applied. The result must necessarily be that the outcome is something far more than Isaias, Osee or Luke, for example, could have produced, precisely as the result of my skilled application of my razor is something far transcending what the razor alone could have produced. Apart from any revelation or inspiration they received, these three writers could have thought and written precisely as they did, for they only wrote—even under Divine Inspiration—according to their respective natures. But in their writings there would have been something lacking. What? Something akin to that which is transiently communicated to my razor when I am actually using it, something which stamps the ultimate effect with the imprint of reason. Now here it is question of the Divine Mind and the Divine Truth. And it is this that is stamped upon Holy Scripture by the fact that the human writers are God's instruments. Without His inspiration they would have produced writings; as applied by Him they produce *Sacred* Writings. As unassisted writers they would have written things that were true as far as the character of each writer would allow; as inspired writers they produce writings which are *divinely* true.[1]

Yet further: there are, as we said, two minds at work. And though one is subordinate to the other it is in no sense suppressed. The human writer will necessarily have his views, his preoccupations, even his prejudices. He will necessarily speak from the standpoint of his own age and his own upbringing. Where these conflict with the truth that God wants to bring out they will not be allowed to come into play. But short of that the human character of the writer will appear at every turn. It is this that

[1] Notice, too, how St. Thomas urges against his doctrine Aristotle's principle that ' the First Cause has more effect on the thing produced by the second cause than that second cause itself ' (*De Causis*, Prop. i.). and that a legitimate conclusion would be that these secondary causes are thus deprived of liberty. But he replies : ' The First Cause is said to have more influence than the second, inasmuch as its efficiency is more intimate and permanent in the effect than is that of the secondary cause. At the same time the resulting effect is more akin to the second cause, since it is through its means that the act of the First Cause is determined to that particular effect.' *De Veritate*, V. ix. *ad* 10m.

makes the transition so extraordinary when we pass, for instance, from Isaias to Jeremias or Ézechiel.

There are two minds at work : the human and the Divine. Consequently there are two meanings : what God meant and what the human writer meant. Not that these are two independent or conflicting meanings, for where one mind is subordinate to another there can be no conflict. But here we must let St. Thomas speak for himself, as his doctrine on the point is the basis of all his exegetical work.

'The Author of Holy Scripture is God, in Whose power it is to attach a meaning not merely to words—as indeed man can do,—but also to things. Hence it is that whereas in all sciences words have a significance, it is the peculiar property of this science (revelation) that the actual things signified by the words have themselves a further significance.

'Consequently the first signification, that namely whereby the words used signify things, belongs to the primary sense, that is the historical or literal sense. But that meaning whereby the things signified by the words do themselves further signify other things is termed the spiritual sense ; and this is based upon the literal sense and presupposes it.

'Now this spiritual sense has a threefold division. For, as the Apostle says,[1] the Old Law is a figure of the New, and the New Law itself is, as Denis says,[2] a figure of future glory. In the New Law, too, those things which are done by our Head are signs of what we also ought to do.

'According then as those things which pertain to the Old Law signify the things of the New Law, we have the *allegorical* sense. And according as those things which were done in Christ—or in the things which were types of Christ—are signs of the things which we ourselves ought to do, so we have the *moral* sense. Finally, according as they signify those things which are in eternal glory, we have the *anagogic* sense.

'The literal sense is that which the author intends ; now the Author of Scripture is God, Who simultaneously comprehends all things in His intellect ; consequently there is no incongruity in holding, as Augustine says,[3] that even according to the literal sense there may be many meanings in one literal passage of Scripture.'

[1] Heb. x. 1.   [2] *De Coelesti Hierarchia*, V. i.
[3] *Confess*. XII. xviii.-xxxii.

And when it is urged that this multiplicity of ' senses '—
the historical or literal, the allegorical, tropological or
moral, and the anagogical or the path to heaven—is likely
to beget confusion, St. Thomas is content to deny this
on the ground that :

' All those " senses " are based on one, the literal ; on the literal
sense alone can we base arguments, and not on things which are
expressed in allegorical fashion, as Augustine says.[1] Nor is
this derogatory to Scripture, for nothing necessary to faith is
given under the spiritual sense without its being manifestly
stated elsewhere under the literal sense.'

He further points out that the literal sense itself is
twofold. For parabolic expressions come under the
literal sense :

' Since words can signify something directly or figuratively.
For the literal sense here is not the figure of speech itself but the
thing figured. Thus when Scripture speaks of the arm of God
it does not literally mean that God has bodily members of this
kind, but it means that which is signified by such members,
viz. operative power.' [2]

This tabulation of the ' senses ' of Scripture is the key
to the whole of St. Thomas' exegetical work. Thus in his
Proemium to his Commentary on *Lamentations* he says :

' The verbal adornments of this Book make it obscure ; it is
written in metrical fashion and decked out with rhetorical devices.
Further, the various figures of speech made use of render it obscure,
as is the case with the rest of the prophetical Books. It is the
task of sacred expositors to unwrap these wrappings of the Holy
Spirit, for, as Augustine says, the Sacred Scriptures are expounded
by the same Spirit that wrote them.' He then points out that
this lament over Jerusalem can be explained either literally, or
according to the moral, or according to the allegorical sense.
Again, when discussing whether the *Canticle of Canticles* can be
expounded of the Church addressing Christ, he says : ' At times
the actual letter seems opposed to this. Still, so far as such
exposition does not wander from the truths of faith, we need not
repudiate it ; for in the Sacred Page we have not merely the
literal sense which runs continuously, but also the mystical sense
which need not be continuous.' [3]

[1] ' What impudent folly for a man to interpret in his own favour some
allegorical remark, unless he can point to manifest testimonies in the light of
which obscure passages may be cleared up ! ' *Ep.* xciii. 24.
[2] *Summa Theol.* I. 1a. x.   [3] *Expositio altera in Canticum, Proemium.*

We are all aware of the extravagant lengths, to which
the search for the deeper or really ' Spiritual ' meaning of
Holy Scripture was carried by the Alexandrian School,
notably in the persons of Clement and Origen. The
latter even went so far as to deny the necessity of any
literal sense at all in certain passages ; the Antiochian
School of exegesis was little else than a protest against
such perverted principles of interpretation. The *via
media* was discovered by such giants as Chrysostom,
Jerome and Augustine. They, while attaching immense,
indeed primary, importance to the literal sense, yet never
repudiated the mystical interpretation. Some passages of
Scripture have only a literal sense, says St. Augustine,[1]
and St. Thomas endorses this.[2] Yet what more wonderful
example of mystical interpretation can you have than
St. Augustine's marvellous parallel between Benjamin and
St. Paul—the ' lupus rapax ' ? [3]

This same *via media* was followed by St. Thomas.
With him the letter comes first. Thus apropos of Christ's
temptation in the desert : He said to Satan, *Thou shalt
not tempt the Lord thy God.* Was He simply refuting him
by quoting Scripture to him ? Or was He insinuating
that He Himself was God ? ' The former opinion,'
remarks St. Thomas, ' is the more literal.'[4] Similarly,
when dealing at great length with the visit of the Magi, he
expounds fully the literal sense, but then adds brief
mystical considerations.[5] Again, when asking whether
all Christ's temptations were in the desert, he remarks :
' the point is that it does not say so.'[6] Once more : on
Satan's taking Christ up on to the Temple ; Solomon had
made three storeys to the Temple ; to which was Christ
taken up ? It matters not, he answers : ' What is certain
is that He did go up.'[7] Similarly on Ezechiel's being
taken in vision to Jerusalem : ' It is clear that things which

[1] *De Genesi ad litt.* I. [2] *Quodl.* VII. 15, *Sed contra.*
[3] *Sermo* xiv. de Sanctis, *i.e. Sermo* cclxxix., *P.L.* XXXVIII. 1275.
[4] *Comment.* on Matt. iv. [5] *Ibid.* ii.
[6] *Ibid.* iv.
[7] *Ibid.*

are narrated simply as having taken place must equally simply be understood as having so taken place.'[1]

St. Thomas, then, does not have recourse to the ' spiritual ' sense merely because he cannot understand the letter, as unfortunately did Origen. For him, as we have seen, the literal sense is the sole foundation of dogma. Hence it is that his Commentaries on the Epistles of St. Paul stand unrivalled for the minuteness with which the intricacies of the text are unravelled. We venture to say that in this respect St. Chrysostom's Homilies on *Romans* and St. Thomas' Commentary on the same Epistle are of greater value for a real understanding of St. Paul's teaching than any Commentaries since written. This will, we are aware, seem a preposterous statement in the eyes of many. Yet we can quote in its partial support the weighty authority of Erasmus who says of St. Thomas:

' To my thinking no recent theologian has shewn an equal diligence, a saner judgment, a more solid erudition. It is to be regretted that he was not equipped with a knowledge of languages and other aids to Biblical studies, since he made such wonderful use of the means which at that period were at his disposal.'[2]

At the risk of wearying, we will attempt an analysis of a portion of St. Thomas' *Introduction* to his Commentary on the Epistles. He opens with a commentary on the words : ' Vessel of election,' in which he portrays the Apostle of the Gentiles in a way which must appeal to and uplift any thoughtful reader. He then proceeds to group the Epistles. His principles will probably seem fanciful to the modern historical commentator who has no conception of the ' spiritual ' sense of Scripture. Nine of the Epistles, he says, are written to the Churches of the Gentiles, four to prelates and rulers, one to the people of Israel. Now the entire teaching they contain is concerned with the grace of Christ, and that may be studied first of all in the Head of the Church, Christ Himself, that is in the *Epistle to the Hebrews*. That grace may next be con-

[1] *De Potentia*, VI. vii. ; ix. *ad* 5m.
[2] *Commentary on the Epistle to the Romans* i. 2.

K

sidered in the Mystical Body of Christ, the Church ; and either in the rulers or in the members of that Body St. Paul treats of the grace of Christ in itself in *Romans*, in its sacramental effects, whether positively or negatively, in *I.-II. Corinthians* and *Galatians*. Lastly, in its main effect, namely unity as instituted—in *Ephesians*, as confirmed—in *Philippians*, as defended—in *Colossians*, against existing persecutors—in *I. Thessalonians*, against future persecutors—in *II. Thessalonians*. In the Epistles addressed to prelates or to rulers, one, *Philemon*, is addressed to a temporal ruler ; the institution of ecclesiastical unity is the theme of *I. Timothy*, its defence against persecutors the theme of *II. Timothy*, he argues against heretics in *Titus*.

No one who is really familiar with these Epistles will deny the singular aptness of these descriptions. Many, however, will say that such treatment is not helpful, and that historical, philological, and even archaeological treatment would be of much more use. Yet St. Thomas does not despise the historical aspect of the Epistles. It has for him, however, quite a secondary value, and he deals with the order of time and place of each Epistle in some thirty short lines. If anyone had remarked to St. Thomas that he had given very little historical detail he might perhaps have drawn attention to the discussion he has now and again on historical details in the Gospels and on the chronology of the Epistles, etc.,[1] but I think he would have answered them in the words he uses in the *Proemium* to his Commentary on *Job*.

' There have been people who thought that Job never actually existed, but that the story is a species of parable constructed as a sort of peg, as it were, on which to hang a discussion on Providence, just as men often put an imaginary question in order to debate about it. Now as far as the teaching contained in the Book goes, it does not make very much difference whether Job really existed or not. But it may be questioned whether this theory is solidly founded. For it certainly seems to run counter to the authority of Scripture, since we read in Ezechiel (xiv. 14) *If these three men :*

[1] *E.g. Lect.* V. on Gal. ii. ; *Lect.* i. on II. Cor. xii. ; *Dedicatory Epistle* prefixed to the *Catena Aurea* ; *Summa Theol.* IIIa., iv. vi. 5.

*Noe, Daniel and Job shall be in the midst thereof they shall deliver
their own souls by their justice.* Now it is clear that Noe and
Daniel did actually exist ; consequently it would seem that there
can be no room for questioning the actual existence of the third
who is named, *viz.* Job. So, too, in Jas. v.: *Behold we account them
blessed who have endured. You have heard of the patience of Job,
and you have seen the end of the Lord.* Consequently we have to
believe that Job was a person who actually existed. But at what
date he lived, and who his parents were, and who it was who
wrote this Book—whether, namely, Job himself wrote it speaking
of himself in the third person, or whether some one else wrote the
Book about Job, it is not to our purpose to discuss here. For all
we aim at here is to give—according to our capacity, and in reliance
on God's assistance—a brief exposition according to the literal
sense of the Book entitled *Of the Blessed Job ;* for the blessed
Pontiff Gregory has with such subtlety and wisdom set forth its
deeper mysteries that nothing can well be added to his work.' [1]

Nothing, then, could be more explicit than St. Thomas'
teaching on the place of allegory and metaphor in Holy
Scripture. For him they are the basis of all true exegesis.
These forms of speech are necessary because of our human
nature, which instinctively argues from the known to the
unknown, from the sensible to the spiritual. But allegories
and metaphors are not used in the Bible as poets use them ;
for these make use of tropes and figures of speech precisely
because they give pleasure, whereas Holy Scripture is
simply seeking to present to us Divine truths in a fashion
which shall best secure our apprehension of them.

' The light of Divine revelation,' he says, ' is not obscured by the
sensible images in which it is enwrapped, but abides in its own
truth. For these figures of speech are used so as to assist the
mind that receives revelation, not simply to abide in such images
but to be uplifted to the knowledge of intelligible truths ; also
that through those who are the recipients of revelation others may
receive fitting instruction concerning it. Hence it is that what
is told in metaphorical guise in one place in Scripture is set forth
more explicitly in other places. Moreover this very veiling of the
truth in figures of speech is profitable for the exercising of studious
minds, and is a safeguard against the gibes of unbelievers.' [2]

[1] St. Thomas' *Prologue* to his *Commentary on Job, Opera Omnia.* Venice, 1675.
[2] *Summa Theol.* Ia. i. 9 ; *cf. Prol.* to *Comment.* on *Lamentations,* also to his second *Comment.* on *Canticles.*

D

St. Thomas' Breadth of Treatment of Biblical Questions

AFTER this it will perhaps come as a surprise to be told that St. Thomas is singularly broad in his actual interpretation of the Bible. Yet such is the case. To take a concrete example. For the Fathers—for St. Basil, St. Gregory of Nyssa, St. Ambrose and St. Augustine, to mention but a few names—the great problem was how to arrive at a sound understanding of the story of creation in Gen. i.-ii. St. Thomas repeatedly sums up their ideas[1] and ranges himself with St. Augustine in opposition to the Greek Fathers. Now a detail which provoked much discussion of old was the precise nature of the ' firmament ' which apparently divided the upper from the lower waters. Some imagined the ' firmament ' was an immense body of water. This notion St. Thomas rejects :

' Since this idea is shewn by many arguments to be false, we cannot say that it is really the meaning of Scripture. We have to reflect that Moses was speaking to an uneducated people ; in condescension to their weakness he only set before them those things which appeared manifestly to their senses.' [2]

Note that he says ' Moses ' not ' God, the principal Author of Scripture.' Again, discussing why the ' lights ' were made, he points out that ' there are various reasons why any created thing is made : it may be made for the sake of some other created thing, or for the part it will play in the universe, or simply for the glory of God ; but Moses, wishful to keep the people from idolatry, only touched upon the reason that these " lights " were useful to men.' [3] The principle that Moses' statements are to

[1] *Summa Theol.* Ia, lxvi.-lxxiv.   *Quaest. Disp. De Potentia,*iv.
[2] *Summa Theol.* Ia, lxviii. 3.
[3] *Ibid.* lxx. 2.

be judged by the intellectual standards of the people for whom he wrote is repeated again and again.[1]

When treating the question whether the Law was given through the ministry of Angels—a question which he decides in the affirmative—St. Thomas raises the difficulty that *The Lord spoke to Moses face to face as a man is wont to speak to his friend*,[2] and that as *the Law was given by Moses*[3] it follows that Moses received the Law directly from God. But he answers that :

' As Augustine says on the words quoted : shortly after it is added *Shew me Thy glory* ; Moses knew then what he saw, what he did not see he yearned to see ;[4] Moses therefore did not see the essence of God and consequently was not directly instructed by Him. When, then, it is said that *God spoke to him face to face*, Scripture is speaking according to the opinion of people who fancied that Moses spoke mouth to mouth with God when, through the medium of some created thing, that is the Angel and the cloud, He spoke to him and appeared to him.'[5]

There is no denying that this is singularly bold exegesis. We have another example, though a less forcible one, in the Saint's treatment of quotations from speakers or actors in the Bible. Thus he quotes, against his doctrine on the efficacy of prayer, the words of the blind man : *We know that God doth not hear sinners ;* but he is content to reply with St. Augustine : ' those are the words of the blind man not yet wholly illumined with wisdom ; consequently they contain a falsehood.'[6] An even more striking instance of the same occurs in the discussion on the immortality of the soul. He puts the objection that *the death of man and of beasts is one, and the condition of them both is equal ; as man dieth so do they also die ; all things breathe alike and man hath nothing more than beast.*[7] His reply is that, ' Solomon brings forward an argument by personating the foolish man, as is suggested in Wisdom ii.

---

[1] *Ibid.* lxvii. 4 ; lxix. 2 ; lxx. 1 *ad* 3m. ; *De Potentia*, iv. 2 *ad* 30m., and *ad* 31m. *Lectio* i. on Job. xxvi.
[2] Exod. xxxiii. 11.   [3] Jn. i. 17.
[4] *De Genesi ad litt.* XII. xxvii. (55), *P.L.* XXXIV. 477.
[5] *Summa Theol.* Ia, 2dae, xcviii. 3 *ad* 2m.
[6] *Tract. in Joann.* xliv. 13 ; *P.L.* XXXV. 1718.
[7] Eccles. iii. 19.

. . . Consequently those words in Ecclesiastes are false.'[1] It is interesting to note how the Saint seems to have anticipated the very modern view that *Wisdom* was written as an antidote to the pessimism of *Ecclesiastes*.

Another instance of the same breadth of treatment is furnished by the summoning of Samuel from the grave by the witch of Endor.[2] St. Thomas first of all points out that the soul of Samuel was not in the enjoyment of the Beatific vision ; secondly, that even so it could only have been by Divine permission that he came back to earth. But he adds : ' It might also be said that it was not the soul of Samuel, but some evil spirit personifying him, and the witch called this Samuel since Saul and the by-standers thought it was so.'[3]

Again, Matthew and Luke give us a different order in the series of Christ's temptations in the desert. St. Thomas quotes St. Augustine : ' It is uncertain which took place first, whether the kingdoms of this world were first shewn to Him and He was then taken up to the pinnacle of the temple, or *vice versa* ; nor does it really matter, so long as it is clear that all these things did take place ' ;[4] and then he himself adds : ' the Evangelists seem to have put things in a different order because sometimes a man proceeds from conceit to covetousness and sometimes it is the other way.' He seems to take it for granted that the inspired Evangelists constructed their narrative on certain moral principles ![5]

Once more, when discussing the details of the Crucifixion[6] he raises the difficulty that whereas St. Luke had said that one of the thieves blasphemed Him, St. Matthew says *the thieves who were crucified with Him blasphemed Him.* St. Thomas sees no difficulty in the explanation given by St. Augustine : ' We can presume that Matthew wrote

---

[1] *Summa Theol.* Ia, lxxv., 6 *ad* 1m.
[2] I. Sam. xxviii. Ecclus. xlvi. 23.
[3] *Summa Theol.* 2da, 2dae, clxxv. 5 *ad* 4m. ; *cf. ibid.* xcv. 4 *ad* 2m., and Ia, lxxxix. 8 *ad* 2m. ; *cf.* St. Augustine, *Ad Simplicianum*, II. qu. iii. 3 ; *P.L.* XL. 144.
[4] *De Consensu Evangelistarum*, II. xvi. (33) ; *P.L.* xxxiv. 1093.
[5] *Summa Theol.* IIIa. xli. 4 *ad* 5m.
[6] *Ibid.* xlvi. 2 *ad* 3m.

the plural for the singular.'[1]   But he adds St. Jerome's
explanation : ' At first both blasphemed Him, but one
of them believed when he saw the signs ' (viz, the earth-
quake, etc.).[2]

The reason for this type of exegesis is simplicity itself :
Holy Scripture—as we have already seen—is meant to
lead us men to God by what it says as well as by what its
words, and the characters who figure in its pages, signify.
True exegesis, then, is bound to bring out this meaning in
all its fullness. To stop at the bare letter is literally to
stop short at the husk. This distinction between the
literal and spiritual sense we have already fully set forth
from St. Thomas' own pages, but in the following passage
he is if anything more explicit :

' Holy Scripture makes manifest to us in two ways the truth it
contains : by words and figurative things. The manifestation
by words constitutes the literal or historical sense. Consequently
whatsoever is correctly deduced from the meaning of the words
pertains to the literal sense. But the spiritual sense, as has been
said, is derived from or consists in the fact that certain things are
expressed through figures of other things : visible things are wont
to be types of invisible things, as Denis says. Hence it comes that
that meaning which is derived from figures is termed " spiritual."
Now the truth which Holy Scripture delivers to us by means of
the figures of things is directed towards two goals : right belief
and right action. If the goal is right action then we have the
moral sense, also known as the tropological. If the goal is right
belief then we have to make a distinction according to the relative
position of the things of faith. For, as Denis says,[3] the position
of the Church is midway between that of the Synagogue and that
of the Church Triumphant. Consequently the Old Testament was
a figure of the New ; and the Old and New Testaments together
are figures of heavenly things. It follows, then, that the spiritual
sense, the goal of which is right belief, can either be based on that
species of figure whereby the Old Testament typifies the New—
and then we have the allegorical or typical sense in accordance
with which the events which took place in the Old Testament are
expounded of Christ and His Church ; or it can be based on that
species of figure whereby the Old and the New Testament alike
signify the Church Triumphant, and then we have the anagogical
sense.

[1] De Consensu Evangel. II. xvi.
[2] On Matt. xxvii.
[3] De Coel. Hierarchia, iv.

' Nor are these four " senses " so attributed to Holy Scripture that every portion of it has to be expounded according to all four ; but sometimes according to all four, at others to three, at others to two, at others according to one only.   For in Scripture, subsequent things are specially typified by what has preceded.   Consequently in Scripture something is sometimes said according to the literal sense about an earlier event which can admit of a spiritual application in the case of later events, but not conversely. Now in all that is narrated in Holy Scripture the first are those which belong to the Old Testament ; consequently those things which, according to their literal signification, have regard to the facts of the Old Testament, can be expounded according to all four senses.   Next come those things which concern the present state of the Church, and here those things come first which concern the Head, relatively that is to the things that concern the members ; for the true Body of Christ Itself, and the things that are done in It, are figurative of the mystical body of Christ and of the things that are done in it ; so that we ought to take Christ Himself as an example of right living.

' But in Christ future glory too is foreshewn us ; consequently the things which are said literally of Christ the Head can be expounded allegorically by referring them to His mystical body, morally by referring them to our acts which ought to be modelled on His example, and anagogically inasmuch as in Christ the path to eternal glory is mapped out for us.

' When, however, something is said about the Church according to the literal sense we cannot expound that allegorically, unless perhaps in the same way as things said about the primitive Church can be expounded as illustrative of the future state of the present Church.   Such things can, however, be expounded morally and anagogically.   Those things, again, which according to the literal sense are moral teachings, are generally only expounded in an allegorical fashion.   Finally, things which according to the literal sense are concerned with the state of glory cannot be expounded in any other way, for the simple reason that such things are not figurative of other things but are themselves prefigured by all other things.'[1]

Enough has been said to shew on what broad and solid lines St. Thomas worked in dealing with the Bible.   The twofold authorship of Sacred Scripture demands the twofold meaning ; all sane exegesis must take both of these into account ; only in this way can the rights of the Principal Cause as well as those of the instrumental causes be fully safeguarded.

[1] *Quodlib*. VII. xv.

EPILOGUE

By the Rt. Rev. Mgr. Gonne

"If any man speak, let him speak as the words of God."
—*I. Peter, iv., 11.*

When the Holy Father wrote last year his Encyclical Letter ' Studiorum ducem ' in which he called upon the faithful to join in commemorating the sixth centenary of the canonisation of St. Thomas Aquinas, he surveyed the position held by the great Doctor in the Schools and Councils of the Church, and finally and definitely enthroned him as the Common or Universal Doctor, ' because his doctrine the Church has made her own.' In issuing this Encyclical, the Pope was, in effect, issuing a challenge to the world of non-Catholic thought and teaching. And never was there a moment more ripe for such a challenge. For everywhere uneasy suspicion holds the hearts of the people. Men and women are resentful over the past and apprehensive of the future. They are disquieted with the results of the materialistic teaching and culture which have held the field so long, and are contemptuous of the claims of science and politics to satisfy the souls of men. Ordinary men and women, whose vision is normally limited to the daily round of events, are beginning to sense dimly what thinkers are seeing clearly, that the confusion and insincerity of the unspiritual world of to-day are the outcome of the false ideals and muddled thinking of the last two centuries. As an eminent Professor of philosophy, non-Catholic, publicly proclaimed this week : ' The bad habit of beginning the study of so-called modern philosophy with Descartes is responsible for generations of mere fumbling in the dark which might have been escaped if the gentlemen of the eighteenth and nineteenth centuries had been willing to do less " sneering at Aquinas " and more study of him.'

Into this arena of turmoil and confusion of thought, this atmosphere of fear and suspicion the Holy Father flung his challenge. He called upon the faithful to make a demonstration of the teaching and philosophy of the

Church as enshrined in the works of her chief Master, Aquinas. Such a demonstration would reveal not merely the secret of the stability of the Church, not merely the sources of her strength and vitality, but would reveal, more in particular, the link of which the world has definitely lost sight, the necessary link between true knowledge and virtue ; ' for true science and genuine piety,' says the Encyclical, ' are linked together in a wondrous kinship,' and further, ' this marvellous fellowship of doctrine with piety, of learning with virtue, of truth with charity was singularly pre-eminent in the Angelic Doctor.'

And the celebrations which, in obedience to the command of the Holy Father, are taking place in nearly every centre of learning throughout the world, have revealed in astonishing manner how deep is the impress of the mind and character of St. Thomas on the daily life of the Church, and, outside the Church, how living his prestige. It was our good fortune that Manchester should be chosen as the centre for our own national celebrations and that our Metropolitan should grace with his presence the final scenes. The choice was one of deep significance. When a University like the University of Manchester, so typically modern, so prolific in scientific research and discovery, so unsentimental over the heritage from the past, so prophetic of the turn and trend of the future ; when a University such as this throws open hospitable doors to large gatherings of cultured people, mainly non-Catholic, that they might hear the message of Aquinas from the lips of non-Catholic leaders of learning, nay, more significantly, from the lips of members of that glorious Order of Blackfriars of which St. Thomas is the pride and glory ; when all this happens in what is, after all, but the springtime of the re-born Church in England, we can say with sober truth that these celebrations mark a definite stage in the Church's struggle for life and recognition in this our country. The Hounds of the Lord, beaten out by the intruder four hundred years ago, are scenting their way back to their native lair, the Universities of England.

It is not now the occasion to expound the teaching of Aquinas ; rather it is the moment to hymn the praise of the Saint. His figure has this past week been painted for us by skilled hands in the light and setting of his achievement, the figure of which the painting in the Spanish Chapel of Santa Maria Novella in Florence is the counterpart, the figure of one raised above the ordinary human plane of existence by the upthrust of his intellectual power and the uplift of his heroic sanctity ; the figure of a supreme architect and master-builder who has reared a cathedral of thought and ideas before which the mightiest material edifice shrinks into insignificance. For the *Summa Theologica* is a work so vastly and nobly planned, so harmoniously constructed, so aptly adjusted part to part and each part to the whole, that it stands for all time the greatest monument of the Middle Ages, resting on piers of solid reason and learning, rising triumphant in column of revealed truth and arch of soaring faith, glorified and illumined by warm, rich colours of moral and mystical teaching.

Mind of tremendous sweep and power, heart of a holy child, that was Aquinas, who whilst meditating profoundly on the unsearchable mysteries of God, could sing them the while in simple, spontaneous, bird-like note—

' Pange, lingua, gloriosi corporis mysterium.'

Or, again, in that heart-shattering paean—

' Lauda, Sion, Salvatorem. . . .
Sit laus plena, sit sonora,
Sit jucunda, sit decora
Mentis jubilatio.'

Never did exalted poetry and profound teaching meet in more ecstatic embrace.

But there is one aspect of the Angelic Doctor which only Catholics can envisage and appreciate—that aspect of him, not as the angel of light, but as the guardian angel of learned Catholic youth. There is a story told of Aquinas how, as a child of six or seven, when he was living at Monte

Cassino, he used to walk about the monastery asking the monks the question, ' Quid est Deus ? '

This is the prime question which the young ecclesiastic in every Catholic College and Seminary throughout the world must ask himself when he embarks upon his philosophical and theological studies.   What is God ?   The answer to that question is momentous and decisive in the lives of all men, but especially of those who are ' called by God, as Aaron was.'   And for answer the Church leads her sons to St. Thomas.   And then it is that the glorious patron of our schools and faculties begins his work of fashioning and nourishing and enriching the minds of ecclesiastical Catholic youth, whether Dominican or Franciscan, Benedictine or Jesuit, foreign missioner or secular, or of any order or congregation of priests.   Was nobler office ever given by God to man ?   The whole Church is the school of Aquinas.   Daily his voice is raised in teaching, and his voice the Church has made her own, calming and satisfying the curious mind of youth with arguments and proofs justly conceived, powerfully reasoned, and nobly expressed.   And when in those all too rare moments of clear insight and vision a priest is privileged after his Mass to apprehend in some measure the dreadful significance of that great Sacrifice, when his heart is overflowing yet mute of expression, it is St. Thomas who voices for him the yearning and satisfaction of his soul.

Unconquerable faith, burning charity, life of chastity, true knowledge, these were the gifts he prized most highly, prayed for most fervently, was given most abundantly. Can they before whom he is held up as Patron of the Schools and Model of the Priesthood do better than make his ideal their own, and pray with him and to him—

> Sancte Thoma Scholarum Patrone,
> Fidem invictam,
> Charitatem fervidam,
> Vitam castissimam,
> Scientiam veram,
> A Deo nobis obtine.

www.ingramcontent.com/pod-product-compliance
Lightning Source LLC
Chambersburg PA
CBHW060349090426
42734CB00011B/2083